Passion for Purity

– principles from a personal journey into wholeness

Susan B. Williams
Peter R. Holmes

JEHOVAH RAPHA: I am the mender, the one who sews you together into Christ (e.g.EX15 :26)

Jehovah
Rapha

Dedication

To the Elders and congregation of Christ Church, Deal, who are turning the truths of this book into living reality in church community.

Copyright © Susan B. Williams and Peter R. Holmes 2000.
The right of Susan B. Williams and Peter R. Holmes to be identified
as authors of this book has been asserted by them in
accordance with the Copyright, Designs
and Patents Act 1988.

First published in 2000 by Discipleship Ltd.,
Waterfront, Kingsdown Road, Walmer, Kent CT14 7LL.

ISBN 0 95380 433 X

All rights reserved.
No part of this publication may be reproduced or
transmitted in any form or by any means, electronic
or mechanical, including photocopy, recording or any
information storage and retrieval system, without
permission in writing from Discipleship Ltd.,
Kingsdown Road, Walmer, Kent CT14 7LL

British Library Cataloguing Data
A catalogue record for this book is available
from the British Library.

Scripture quotations in this publication are mainly
from the NIV version of the Bible published by
Hodder & Stoughton Ltd

Photos: Ian Giles, Deal - with thanks.

Book design production for the publishers by
Gazelle Creative Productions,
Concorde House, Grenville Place, Mill Hill, London NW7 3SA.

Contents
and Index of Teaching Pieces

Preface	7
Introducing The Book	9
1. Hope For Wholeness	11
Becoming New Creatures?	15
Why Our Pasts Affect Our Future	17
Our Spiritual House	21
Jehovah Rapha	22
2. Healing Begins	25
The Spiritual World	26
Feeling Is Healing	28
Knowing Christ Is Knowing Truth About Ourselves	30
Becoming The Person God Created You To Be	33
Loving Oneself	34
Life As Humility And Sonship	36
Spiritual Surgery	37
3. A Blockage	41
Christians And The Demonic	42
Sin Against Oneself	46
Hearing The Voice Of God	48
Being Hurt By Others Without Realising It	50
Bloodline Sin	51
4. Breakthrough	53
Repentance And Spiritual Knowledge	54
Trusting	57
Being Healed But Feeling Wobbly	60
Foretaste Of Healing	64
Scripts	67
The Deceit Of Control	70

5. Recovery And Release — 73
- Families And Our Healing — 76
- Living With The Spiritual Dimension — 80
- Spiritual Body Language — 84
- Christ And Satan — 88

6. Introducing 'Inner Healing' — 91
- Possessing Healing — 92
- Righteous And Unrighteous Emotion — 94
- Revenge — 98
- Saying Good-Bye — 100
- Homework — 101
- Sleep — 104

7. Women And The Spiritual World — 105
- Do We Ever Come To An End Of Healing? — 105
- What Is Sin? — 107
- Honouring Parents — 109
- The Companionship Of Baggage — 111
- Lordship — 112
- Deepest Darkness Just Before The Dawn — 114
- Repenting On Behalf Of Others — 115
- God-Man-Woman — 118

8. Traumatic Memories — 120
- Being Healed But Empty — 120
- Guidance — 124
- Self Curses — 128
- Sexual Abuse — 131

9. Healing And Brokenness — 137
- Walking With Christ — 138
- The Gender Continuum — 140
- Our False Selves — 145
- What Is Brokenness? — 148
- The Journey Into Maturity — 150
- Life And Death — 152

10. The Purpose Of Healing — 155
- Our Stolen Spiritual Potential — 156

Preface

When Susan Williams, gaunt, ghost-like and full of fear stepped for the first time over the threshold of our home in Bromley on January 1st 1988, neither my wife Mary, or I knew the true significance of what was beginning. It birthed a journey we are all still on. But I was not surprised to see her. The reason was most interesting.

It was probably the Spring of 1983 that I saw her walking down the church steps one Sunday morning. At the time Mary and I were part of the youth leadership team and Susan had been on the sick list for some time. I looked at her as the Lord told me to pray for her, telling me, 'This woman will be fully healed by Me for My glory.' I continued to pray as He requested until the day we met in 1988. Some years later I shared this with her and she knew the moment. Although she didn't know who I was, she had felt me looking at her. So it was 1983 when the journey really began for all of us.

Susan has always been different to the many others I have ministered to. No-one ever asked me as many questions as Susan did. She always needed me to explain how I *knew* what I did. She needed to know *how* and *why* it worked. Likewise no-one else had ever quizzed me on the Biblical background or the reasons I suggested the approach I did for her journey into wholeness. She has never stopped asking questions. In the early days it was driven by need, but in time simply because she knew it worked and wanted to learn the 'how-to' for herself. Her testimony, piles of journals and her diaries testify to her desire to understand

the ways of the Lord in healing her and also all those who subsequently have come to her.

As she learned, so she shared with others. One of the outcomes was she encouraged me to write up some of my observations about growth in discipleship and wholeness. We began to call these papers 'Bible Notes'. We made them available, where appropriate, to others seeking help. Most of the boxes in the testimony are very brief summaries of these notes, now well over 100. As the numbers of people coming for ministry increased, these notes also helped us avoid saying the same things over and over again! Enquirers and the notes have continued to come in larger numbers. So much so that folk all over the UK and further afield began to contact us, seeking help and inviting Susan to teach the simple principles the Lord had taught her.

We began asking how we could help all these 'friends of friends' coming to our door. After some thought we began 'Workshops for Women'. We ran the first one for twenty-five women over three days here in our home in Walmer in late 1998 and so, almost by accident our workshop ministry was born. At the time of writing over 500 women have been through these Workshops somewhere here in the UK and the USA, and the ministry is now being extended to men. It continues to grow.

All this has happened because Susan was so desperate she declared to the Lord she was willing to let Him heal her any way He chose. He did so by taking her on a meticulous spiritual adventure through deep layers of knowing both herself and her God. She learned every lesson well. He answered her with her healing and gave us all so, so much more.

Peter R. Holmes
Christ Church, Deal, UK
Spring 2000

Introducing The Book

Because this book has taken so many years to write, it now consists of both historic narrative of Susan's journey into maturity in Christ, but also a number of boxes summarising teaching that for Susan proved a matter of life and death. The book is therefore not a quick read, but is intended to be a *meditative journey* for all those who wish to know why they have still not found what they are looking for in Christ.

The wider church is in crisis since on the whole we have proven unable to bring maturity in Christ to those we have won. The more damage people have in their lives the less likely it is the church can help them. Therefore many who enter the front door of our churches limp out by the side exit within a few years, often departing even more sick and embittered through encountering the church. This is an appalling scandal and we as Christians, particularly leaders, should be looking again at why we are unable to bring wholeness to those Christ specifically came to save (Mark 2:17).

Jesus came to heal the sick and in one sense we are all sick from the disease called sin. But many in our society are unable to even function under the normal routines of life, held back by the hidden evil of their damaged pasts. Discipleship should be taught as a letting go of our pasts in order to possess a future of wholeness in Christ. As a church we have still not learned to turn human dysfunctionality into an asset, by teaching folk how to *meet Jesus*. We believe

---

Handwritten note: When JESUS heard it, HE said to them, "Those who are well have no need of a physician but those who are sick. I did not come to call the righteous but sinners to repentance."

Margin: Jehovah Rapha

we must all relearn the simple desire of the Father to bring wholeness to us all by *knowing* and *listening* to His Son in a personal way.

This is, therefore, not a simple book about Susan's healing from sickness, but about the Saviour who leads us by a journey away from our sin-sick pasts, who turns our sicknesses into wholeness. In Christ Church, Deal and our Workshops in Europe and North America we are finding that the simple principles mentioned in this book, along with many others we are recovering, are having a remedial impact on human disorder way beyond even our expectations. We are learning that when a person meets Jesus and begins hearing His voice clearly for themselves, the past, like clinging rotten grave-clothes, seems to fall away. This is what discipleship should be for all of us. Taking the dysfunctional reality of our sinful lives and through both hearing Jesus for ourselves and the social process of living truth before one another, becoming endowed by Christ with the mature wholeness we all so lack.

Susan's journey required she first admit she was ill, then seek with the Lord's help to expose the hidden reasons why she was so sick. She did this by listening to the Lord, finding Christ to be sufficient as she acted in obedience to Him. This was all very simple, looking back, but at the time involved huge battles. It is our prayer that this journey and its book may give hope to some of those lost in the maze of their own problems, pointing a way out to a person who is closer than a brother, if we are willing to give time to finding Him. This book is not about healing, but about *meeting Jesus* and by our own *passion for purity* finding the wholeness we all so desperately need.

Susan B. Williams
Peter R. Holmes
Walmer, UK.

1 *Hope For Wholeness*

The Lord does not want to teach you to cope with your problems. He wants to heal you. In my twelve years of being a Christian, I had never heard anyone say that to me. And what was more astonishing, was that it was clear this man really did believe it. Although I had barely met Peter, there was a spontaneous trust (tinged with fear) that rose in me.

I was huddled on the mediaeval-style couch of Peter and Mary Holmes in their home in Bromley on the outskirts of South London. The previous week, quite independently of each other, two friends in different parts of the world had telephoned me to say that the only man they knew who could help rescue me from a second nervous breakdown was Peter Holmes. I was too ashamed of my failed Christianity to contact anyone else, but Peter rang and invited me over for Sunday tea.

I was twenty-seven. My first 'nervous breakdown' at the age of twenty-one and its subsequent agoraphobia had kept me away from full-time employment for two years and I knew I could not endure all that trauma again. I was within days of being forced back to my psychiatrist, admitting that my 'healing' had not worked after all and I needed to be put back on the anti-depressants and tranquillisers I had stopped three months before. Admission to a psychiatric ward felt virtually inevitable and I knew I would not ever want to come out again.

So it was with great shock that I found myself believing

Peter's promise. But what I didn't believe was the caution that followed it; 'The journey of healing will be worse than the hell you are in.' I remember few other details of that afternoon. I went off that evening to speak at a church meeting. Ironically the subject was 'loving yourself', something I knew a huge amount about in my head but was utterly incapable of applying to my personal life. I survived the evening without anyone discovering the double life I was living as I retreated back to my personal hell to consider Peter's words. He would not accept a decision from me on the spot but required I think it through with the Lord for a minimum of a week before coming back to him. But I knew what my answer would be. He was my last stop before insanity or suicide. No choice really.

Imagine your life like a palatial mansion, every room radiant with life, vivid colour and intense reality. Too good to be true? When Christ stepped into my life, I didn't even know I had a spiritual house and I was certainly oblivious to its contents. But ten years later its barren darkness was barely hidden in my busyness. Most rooms in my mansion had been locked up for so long they were neglected and damp. I had lost the keys and forgotten the rooms even existed. My life was confined to the servant's quarters in the basement I called home, leaving my mansion in such decay that its condition was a constant problem to me. But God was precipitating a crisis which was now exposing these ruins in my spirit. He wanted to take me to every area of my life which was not full of Life and transform it, releasing me into a wholeness I never dared believe was possible. I'm no-one special. We all have such a mansion which God is eager to help us reclaim. This is my personal journey.

* * *

My childhood years gave me no clue that I would need such deep healing, for my life had seemed very ordinary. I am the eldest of three girls and was brought up in a South London suburb. My father's family were working class Londoners. My mother's were more wealthy and from out of town. Although both mum and dad had parents with difficult marriages, our home displayed no evidence of such damage. In fact, we seemed very 'normal' and I had no reason to think our family life was anything but happy. With my sisters I went regularly to a church selected because of the wide range of social activities it held for children. My parents attended on special occasions. I did not make friends easily, so would have preferred not to participate, but as I was not given the choice I succeeded well in what I tried. As a child I remember saying the Lord's prayer privately and reverently at night, but it was all I knew of God.

To an outsider there would have been some evidence that all was not well. I was painfully shy and clearly fearful of any situation which was unfamiliar. I am told I was excessively well-behaved as a little girl, not even having temper tantrums. I didn't like wearing dresses and would rather play with the boys. One of my biggest childhood upsets was the day I discovered Father Christmas didn't exist! By eleven years of age I could have scraped into the local High School, but opted for Grammar School instead, where I worked hard for the modest success I achieved. Only in music did I seem to have a natural aptitude, although my fear ensured I would never excel.

I became a Christian when I was fifteen at an outdoor pursuits holiday in Scotland that I had been taken to by a school friend. For the first time I saw young people enjoying themselves in a way I had never known. They said it was because of their relationship with Jesus and I decided I

wanted what they had. However, within hours of this decision I had my first (and only) asthma attack, so severe I was given immediate medication and had to have someone with me twenty-four hours a day. It kept me from the sailing, climbing and water-skiing I had wanted to try – I was grounded. So with nothing better to do I read the various Christian books that were lying around and bought my first Bible. On returning home I temporarily suffered several other inexplicable sicknesses, but these did not stop me pursuing my new-found faith with studious enthusiasm. During the following months I began to understand what sin was, why Jesus died and the implications of my decision to follow Him. My family moved to Bromley, a London borough on the edge of Kent and I became an active member of a local evangelical church, joining the youth group and helping to lead the Christian Union at school. From being quiet and introverted, I began to grow in confidence. I had a reputation for laughing loudly and discovered to my surprise that leadership came naturally to me.

But I also grew in my awareness that I appeared to be different from other people. In public I was now more gregarious and able to enthuse others, yet on my own I was often sad, fearful and struggling in my relationship both with the Lord and people. I suffered from depression, although I did not realise this, dealing with my misery privately. In honest moments I admitted the joy I had sought in becoming a Christian was not there. Walking home from school one day I confessed to a friend that 'the hardest thing about loving your neighbour as yourself, isn't loving your neighbour – it's loving yourself'. It was the closest I was to come for some time to one of the main symptoms of the deep problems I really had.

Becoming New Creatures?

Jesus tells us we are 'born-again' and a new creation. But I was to learn that in my case the reality of this transformation had not all happened at conversion. Some Christians teach that if we do not get rid of all our problems and sicknesses when we come to Christ we are either living in sin, lack faith or have something else wrong with us. Yet many of my physical and emotional sicknesses actually began or worsened at my conversion and I have since met many Christians with similar difficulties. I am delighted for those folk who have genuinely had all their troubles taken away when they become Christians. But God was to take me on a painfully different path; although He had made me new, possessing that wholeness as a daily reality was to prove a long and hard journey, not merely an event complete at conversion.

I left school with just enough qualifications to go to college in London. I continued in youth group leadership, together with several other church responsibilities. Much to my surprise I was asked to represent London on a national committee for Christian Unions in colleges, so I began travelling and doing some teaching. I grew in my desire to love the Lord and serve Him with my life. In my studies I was doing very well and outside college my life was a whirl of Christian activity. I was busy for God and found myself good at all that I tried.

However, in the final year of my degree things began to go seriously wrong. My boyfriend and I had split up some months before and I was devastated. Then another broken relationship at church left me feeling totally isolated, confused and shamed. Overnight I spiralled into a deep depression which lasted for several months. I dropped out of all relationships, activities and responsibilities. I left for college

in the morning, faking my usual routine, but wandered the streets of London unable to face home or lectures. I'd arrive late at church, hide at the back and leave before anyone could talk to me. I cried a lot and began to admit I could see no reason to live. I also realised my unexpected condition was out of all proportion to the event that seemed to have triggered it. No-one I knew had experienced anything like it before. I wanted to die.

The curate at church gave me a lot of support during these months. Slowly, as I grew in understanding of the betrayal which had so upset me and began to identify the turmoil of feelings associated with it, I recovered a little. Although I dropped grades at college, I managed to complete my degree in sociology and at church I tentatively began to attend one or two meetings again. I was welcomed into a small worship group, where several of the members had some understanding of the emotional trauma from which I was recovering. And to my amazement the Lord provided a wonderful job in a management position at a London teaching hospital. I loved it and quickly began to excel, even stepping into my boss's shoes when she left very suddenly. My life seemed to be coming back together again. But it was not to last.

Six months after starting work I had a serious 'nervous breakdown'. The foundations of my life had been very rocky and I could hold myself together no longer. For no apparent reason I walked out of work one day, mid-morning, oblivious to what I was doing, went to a friend's house and started crying hysterically. I could not stop. I was prescribed anti-depressants and tranquillisers to stabilise my 'condition' but nevertheless withdrew into a dark and deep isolation and for most of the next three months I stayed in bed and slept in a darkened room, day and night. I often thought of killing myself. I was not allowed visitors.

From being active in many areas of church and profes-

sional life, succeeding in all that I did, my world had suddenly completely collapsed. How come? An attack of the Enemy? My own sin? A metabolic imbalance? I never stopped to question why it happened. I was too obsessed with trying to survive and find a way out. I didn't lose my faith. I continued to believe God existed and Jesus had died for me, but God was something of an irrelevance because of the intensity of my personal problems. I concluded there was obviously something seriously wrong with *me*. I was taken regularly to a Christian psychiatrist, but the trauma it provoked was so intense that in the end I was referred on to an NHS consultant.

Why Our Pasts Affect Our Future

It was such a relief years later to discover that there were reasons for my sicknesses. I learnt that typical of most of us, I had been unwittingly dragging my past into my future. This was creating a complex of deep conflict that had become increasingly intolerable to manage and live 'above'. The choices I was making to walk God's way were colliding with many pockets of pain, fear, hate, etc. from my past, making my life a permanent battle zone. We can all be impacted by three major areas from our past; our own personal sin and disorder; the actions of others against us; and our bloodline. I was to discover that each area contributed significantly to my sickness.

My recovery was hindered by a long battle with agoraphobia – a terrible dread of public places or open spaces. I felt intense fear at the thought of leaving the house and to start with I could not even look out of the window or open the door without being overwhelmed with waves of trauma. I also found it impossible to be around people.

After several months I was advised by my doctors to

leave home as I was not recovering. If necessary, they emphasised, they would admit me to a psychiatric ward. Thankfully, a South African family from the worship group at church graciously invited me to live with them, even though I was still so sick. That was provision indeed. I began to emerge from hiding and learnt to relate to a few people. It took much effort to hold a conversation with just one person. Over the next several months I had help from psychiatrists and psychotherapists, as well as counselling from friends at church. I also had intensive behavioural therapy to overcome my agoraphobia. Each month I thought I would be back at work within weeks, although it was two years before I was to return to full-time employment.

One of my biggest struggles was with church. I was desperate to attend, but each time I tried I was overcome by fear. Many had prayed for me faithfully in my absence during those two years, but even on my return I found it really hard to cope. Taking communion provoked inexplicably terrible feelings of trauma and panic. Social situations were also agony, my only respite being the safety of the small worship group of which I continued to be part.

I worked really hard at recovering from my 'sickness' and with a lot of help, I succeeded. I began doing very well in my NHS job again, first part-time and then when I could handle public transport, full-time. Over the next two years my life began resuming its hectic activity and my relationship with the Lord grew daily until once again it appeared alive and vibrant. Slowly I even began to take up some responsibilities in the church. Although I never sought a reason for my sickness, it seemed the Lord was using it. I found myself able to love, understand and help others in a new way.

At the age of twenty-seven the only remnant of my trauma, other than a residue of fear, appeared to be the

anti-depressants and tranquillisers I was still being prescribed. I thought nothing of this until my father suddenly died and I instinctively doubled the dose just to cope. I excused the extra medication as a normal reaction while I helped my family through the funeral. I had never come so close to death before, but needed to put on a brave face and be strong for everyone else.

Several weeks later I realised I was finding it hard to reduce my pills to their previous level. I casually mentioned to my psychiatrist that I now wanted to stop taking them altogether. He looked nervous, said this would take a minimum of two years and I would find it very difficult. Instead, he suggested, I should resign myself to taking them for the rest of my life; 'Think of them like blood pressure pills that your body needs.' I walked away from his office in shock. I had always thought of myself as fairly intelligent, but it had never occurred to me that I was addicted to these little blue pills I had been popping five times a day for five years. I was horrified. Somewhat impulsively I resolved with God's help to try and find a way to stop taking the drugs.

At this same time I also decided to take my first holiday since leaving college five years earlier. I plucked up the courage to accept an invitation from the friends with whom I had stayed to enjoy spring in South Africa. It was my first trip abroad alone and the first time I had ever flown. It proved a God-given provision. With the support of my friends and some medical supervision I came off the tranquillisers 'cold turkey'. It was quite a battle, full of pain and I would not recommend it to anyone. But I had not expected healing without pain – just that the Lord would walk with me in this pain. He did not fail me. The last vestige of my breakdown was gone... so I thought.

I came back sun-tanned to an English winter, feeling really well. The withdrawal symptoms from the tranquillisers were quite severe and did not ease as I had expected, but

nevertheless I continued 'in faith' to testify to God's goodness in bringing such healing. The Lord did not seem to mind that I assumed I was healed, but He knew the discovery of the truth was going to be a very painful shock. Looking back, I can see that the holiday in South Africa helped prepare the way for my healing. It was an appropriate beginning. The real problem was that I thought that was the end of it. I felt a new lease of life and was more excited that Christmas than ever before. I decided I would look for a new job and felt ready for more responsibility. When I heard that I had to leave the flat I was renting, I even began to consider buying a place of my own.

However to my dismay over the next three months the signs of my illness began reappearing. I became excessively tense and could not stop my fingers twitching and in spite of a very full schedule I could only sleep two or three hours a night. I was very confused and began to sense an unwelcome depression returning. I went to a Christian Harley Street doctor who told me it was stress and I should practice relaxation. It sounded uncomfortably familiar. Reluctantly I admitted this felt just like the build-up to another breakdown. In shame I hid my struggles from everyone, including those at church. They had all tried to help so much. The few I confided in told me that everyone had problems and I had to cope with mine. I should just stop being so introverted. So I tried even harder and buried the truth below my familiar masks. But the conflict became worse and worse. Only with one or two very close friends did I share how desperate I was becoming. Vainly I clung to the fading belief that this was only drug withdrawal – until a pharmacologist from church disagreed with me and told me to make a new appointment with my psychiatrist.

My healing hadn't worked. Again I didn't blame God. I had personally failed. I would have to go back to taking pills, just to survive. But I felt this would be giving up and

represented the slippery slope to admission into a psychiatric ward. I knew drugs were not the answer and to take them again was to admit defeat. For me it represented the end of any hope of real life. In experiencing a breakdown the first time, I never fully accepted how sick I was, but to face it a second time, knowing what was ahead... I knew I could not endure it again. I had become very good at living a lie, but the strain was now proving intolerable. I was in total despair. With no explanation for my sickness, I knew I had no hope whatsoever of any future.

Our Spiritual House

I did not know at the time that my life was like a house which the Lord had entered at conversion. He was able to take over some of the rooms. But others were full of historic damage and disorder which resisted His holy presence. I had to let Jesus in to clean out these rooms. But He required that I go in with Him, sift through the contents and actively co-operate in the healing. This is the journey into holiness or sanctification and continues for our entire life. But as we mature in Christ (not just in years!) He seeks to take over more of our house and will then begin to show the fruit of this as Christ-like spiritual authority, gifting and its anointing. I was to learn that only as I let go of my past would I be able to become the woman He created me to be.

It was in this state that I was introduced to Peter and Mary Holmes and their nine-year-old son, Christopher. Unbeknown to me we had worshipped at the same church for several years when I was in the throes of my first breakdown. Peter had met me, though I had no recollection of ever meeting him. They had been in full-time Christian work for some years and then gone into business. But Peter's 'hobby' for the previous twenty years had been to

seek ways to help those with stubborn emotional and mental illness find their way through it by meeting Jesus and hearing Him talk to them. I was about to be introduced to a model of discipleship or maturing in Christ that would save my life.

I was relieved that I did not need to provide a long explanation to them. Almost right away they said they could help me. And then they made their radical declaration – that the Lord wanted to heal me. Amazing! This promise was like a refreshing spring bringing life to the parched barrenness of my crippled life.

They suggested that if I said 'Yes' to the Lord and His conditions for my healing, Jesus would meet and help me. It would result in release from my past, but I first had to understand the truth about that past. They seemed to know that what was to be revealed to me would be very hard for me to understand and deal with. At that time I also did not appreciate the remarkable significance of this meeting for Peter. He had apparently been praying for my healing for six years but little realised he would himself be part of God's answer.

Jehovah Rapha

'I am the Lord that heals you' (Exodus 15:26) is a favourite verse of many Christians. But I was to learn a new meaning to this ancient text. The Hebrew root for 'rapha' actually refers to 'stitching together a piece of torn cloth'. And although most English translations simply use the word heal, the full meaning of the promise is that the Lord wants to 'sew us back together' so that we can be one whole. But not just within ourselves. We also are to be 'sewn back into Him' as well. This is His promise: that He will heal our fragmented lives while we are also being sewn into Him. God gives this promise conditionally. We must be willing to see ourselves as God sees us, and act on this knowledge

> as God requires. Put another way, the verse reads; 'I am the mender, the one who sews you together into Christ.'

That afternoon Peter and Mary asked me directly whether I was a quitter, or whether I was prepared to see the matter through. They said they would commit themselves to my healing, providing I was willing to do it the Lord's way. They promised that the Lord wanted to restore the years that had been stolen. Even though I still did not really know what my healing involved, I knew I had no alternative. I felt this was my last hope. Peter told me later that during the afternoon, as I curled up in the corner of the long couch, he had seen over and around me stretching out above and behind me, all the issues that had to be addressed. But even then we all thought of a journey of maybe a few months, not several years.

I did not realise how extensively the Lord would need to undo the person I had become in order to release real freedom and life to me. He seemed to have no intention of just patching me up. If I was willing He would release me to be the person He had created me to be. That was what I wanted and from then on it became my daily prayer. I was very frightened at the prospect of discovering the reasons for my sickness and had no clue what it would involve, but in my desperation I chose to seek the Lord's way of healing and to trust Peter and Mary. In hindsight I am grateful that the Lord waited until I was at a complete end of myself, for I had no choice but to abandon myself to His intervention regardless of the pain involved and the undoing of all my preconceptions and prejudices.

As I was in temporary accommodation and knowing how difficult the next few months were to be, Peter and Mary invited me to live with them for as long as I was seeking healing. But they also made it clear that if at any time I

no longer wanted to pursue my healing, they would help me find somewhere else to live. They wanted to offer me every support, but they also knew I would find it impossible to be around them if I stopped being obedient to God in the healing journey. And so my 'undoing' began. I began the journey with the Lord of investigating my abandoned house.

2 *Healing Begins*

With great fear and trepidation I moved in to live with Peter, Mary and Christopher in their large Victorian house in Crescent Road, Bromley. To my horror one of the first things they told me to do was to clear my diary. As well as managing a department of 200 NHS staff in London by day, I was booked up every evening for the next three weeks. Activity had been an unconscious survival mechanism to enable me to run from the pain of my inner turmoil. Never in my life had I let people down by cancelling a commitment – what would they think? It was very hard to do. But Peter and Mary made it clear that healing takes time. If I was not willing to make my healing my priority, then it would not happen.

Suddenly I began to feel very vulnerable. I had no place to hide. My fear intensified. All the props I had used to support the lie that I was OK were being taken away. I was being exposed. It was essential of course, for God requires we be vulnerable to Him. But it was still very traumatic.

I took comfort in the suggestion there were explanations for my sickness. Peter taught there was part of me, my human spirit, of which although I was not yet consciously aware, would be a significant contributor to my illness. My spirit was the part of my human make-up made in God's image that would live eternally when my body died. I found a measure of dignity in the concept that if some of my sickness was hidden to me in my human spirit, which I hadn't yet found – no wonder I wasn't healed! Drugs had helped bury my pain, luring me into thinking the problems no longer existed. Also, no psychological diagnosis would

have recognised that the roots of my sickness had a spiritual dimension, especially since the spiritual world on the whole is closed to modern medicine and even the church.

The irony was that I had no idea what would be there if I did find my human spirit, my spiritual house as I began calling it. I was only just beginning to accept the principle that the tranquillisers had allowed me to blank out parts of who I was. I had not known what I was running away from all the years of my Christian life. I had taken no time to look and knew nothing about the spiritual world, let alone its impact on me. Although on Biblical grounds I could not deny it existed, I guess I felt it was a dangerous place where demons had control, therefore not somewhere I wanted to be.

The Spiritual World

As Christians we all live in two parallel worlds, spiritual and physical. Scripture teaches these two worlds live within each other. The spiritual world, where God dwells, is the home of all spiritual beings, angelic and evil. But we ourselves are also spiritual beings, though the lowest on this hierarchy. For unlike other spiritual creatures we are 'embodied' – that is, we have a physical body as well as a human spirit. Our human spirit is the bridge to this spiritual world. We therefore also live in the spiritual world, whether we are conscious of it or not, and consequently we are all vulnerable to its activities. This is why our Lord gave us spiritual gifts, particularly discernment, so we will not be spiritually blind as we go through life. We must learn as mature Christians how to be at ease both in His world, the spiritual world, as much as we already are in this, the physical world.

My first session with Peter and Mary started more like a chat. They asked me to imagine my mother sitting in the

empty chair opposite. What did I feel...? It seemed such a stupid thing to ask. I didn't feel anything. After a few minutes I began to conclude that perhaps Peter was not going to be as helpful as I thought. But he continued to ask the question – what did I feel? Suddenly the strangest thing happened. I became really cold, curled up in the corner of the couch and said, 'I want to die.' It wasn't just words, the feelings were totally overwhelming... That was the end of the session.

I was stunned. I had begun my journey. My head said that what had happened was ridiculous. I didn't know that feeling was there. Yet I couldn't deny its all-consuming reality – I was shocked that I felt that way about myself. That night they invited me to a production of C.S. Lewis's 'Voyage of The Dawn Treader'. Every scene seemed to depict the journey I feared I was just beginning.

The following day, as I came out of the shock of that first session, I began badgering Peter with questions. What, how, why...? He and Mary offered to pray with me if I was willing to go back to the feelings, but the feelings had all disappeared again, as if by magic! I could not find them. What I did not realise was that an almighty battle had begun between my self-control (aided and abetted by the years of self-denial and the drugs) and the truth the Holy Spirit wanted to reveal to me.

After several days I was really frustrated at the lack of progress. I asked them to help me again. They did and the result was shocking! I started groaning and burping, feeling intense pressure throughout my body. I wanted to scream but nothing came out, although I was writhing in pain. I had no words for the mass of feelings throbbing through me, although anger, fear and hate could accurately describe the assault. I was in terrible conflict. Even as I touched the pain my mind told me to stop making such a fool of myself. And yet I was deeply relieved that I had successfully

unlocked the door to my feelings. I was determined to press on and not hold back. Wave after wave of emotion flooded me and I could feel my muscles clenching with the trauma of engaging such strong feelings.

Feeling Is Healing

Like many in the church I believed a lie, that my emotion is untrustworthy and should be repressed. But the Lord began to teach me, He desired to speak to me through my emotion, to use my feelings to communicate His truth regarding myself and other people. I discovered my feelings were rooted in my human spirit while expressed in my body, and so could be the channel for release of spiritual gifting and holiness. I therefore needed to welcome my emotion and its cleansing, allowing God to take the pain. The Lord wanted to give me life through my feelings. I could not lock the painful emotion away and just keep enjoyable emotion in my daily life and relationship with the Lord. We only have one bouquet of emotion and if any area is contaminated, this affects all. Without our cleansed emotion we are incapable of Life. We worship a passionate God and to do so we must let go of all the toxic personal emotion gathered from our past. Feeling was to become one of my pathways to healing.

The session lasted an hour or so and I guess I would have just gone on and on if it hadn't been for my body calling abruptly for a truce. With one particularly intense wave of pain my shoulder and neck muscles went into spasm, locking my head onto my shoulder. Peter and Mary, who had been urging me to take a break, then insisted that I did so. I assumed the pain would ease in the next few minutes... or the next hour... or at least by the beginning of the next day. But no. When I got up on Sunday morning my head was

'stuck' to my left shoulder. I was terrified. This was healing? What had I done? While Peter went to church with Christopher, Mary took me for my first ever visit to an osteopath for an emergency appointment. Three days later enough trauma had been released from my neck to allow me to wear a surgical collar, which stayed with me for the next three weeks. It was slightly embarrassing trying to explain to my work colleagues how I had hurt myself. Looking back I still chuckle at the impetuous way I insisted on getting on with my healing. I should have taken Peter's advice and done several sessions instead of trying to complete my healing in one. The operation was a success – even though the patient nearly died during surgery!

Thus I was introduced to some of my true feelings – many different emotions which I had locked away whilst growing up. I learnt that just because I did not immediately feel a feeling, that did not mean it was not there. I had many feelings which I could not feel, simply because I did not want to experience them. I felt very little emotion before the healing began other than intense turmoil and depression. But this session had been the evidence of a seething cauldron of accumulated though hidden emotion. Over the next few weeks the Holy Spirit was to expose various feelings to me so I could let them go. At the beginning I could not identify these individually, as they were far too intensely bound together. But gradually I recognised grief, then anger, then the pain of rejection...

As I found these feelings, in obedience to the Lord, I let them flood me. It was intensely physically and emotionally painful. My whole perception of who I had been during my childhood and as a teenager began to dissolve. My naive, sincere and yet deluded Christian life during the previous ten years began suddenly to look empty and barren. Everything I had taken to be 'normal' had to be re-evaluated in the light of what God was showing me through my

feelings. The Lord knew that if I was to receive real healing, I had first to discover the truth about the person I had become. On almost all occasions the truth revealed by Him was radical, even revolutionary to me. It turned my life and thinking upside down, as I discovered the hidden drives and motives behind so many of my thoughts and actions. I was appalled at how deceived I had been about myself. Instead of being a Godly, loving, committed Christian, I found fear, anger, hate, arrogance, shame and guilt. Inside, in the core of my being I was someone very different to the person I had spent my life trying to be. And trying to live the lie against the drive of all my baggage had nearly killed me.

Knowing Christ Is Knowing Truth About Ourselves

Many of us as Christians live a lie. The Enemy has deceived us into believing things about ourselves and our lifestyle that are not true – not true that is from God's perspective. Jesus is Truth and knowing Him means we must be willing to know the truth about ourselves. God promises to tell us, but only as we invite 'the truth, the whole truth and nothing but the truth'. At all times the Lord will retain the right to choose how much to reveal. But every time He does He will be testing us, to see whether we are faithful or prideful about applying this truth to our lives. He frequently brings truth first through our feelings, side-stepping our minds, which will often be 'the devil's playground'. We must strive with God to show we can be trusted with His truth. My healing began when I started to see myself as God saw me.

I found myself feeling increasingly 'undone' as more of my life, with all its misunderstandings, was exposed and cleaned out. I had tried so hard to be the person I should be, but all I had really done was bury the person I really

was. I needed repeated reassurance that 'undoing' the damage was necessary, in order for the Lord to establish a new foundation of wholeness. I was later to understand that the Lord was deliberately and of necessity leading me through historic feelings. But each time I touched into them, the feelings were being permanently removed from my life by Him – His comprehensive alternative to my own attempts at managing, controlling and hiding them. It felt like the same road I had walked during my breakdown, the landmarks were all too familiar, but now I began to see I was moving in the opposite direction! Consistently throughout these months the Lord was teaching me He had no intention of building on a weak and fake foundation. He intended to transform it, removing all the toxic rot, replacing it with Himself. I had to unpack and feel all this painful emotion in order to let it go forever. This meant letting Him show me the lies I believed while welcoming His truth.

I began discovering the contents of my spiritual house. It was as if the Lord had shown me several doors to rooms from my past, taken me in and was now beginning to sort through the contents. Much of it was 'baggage' – damage and disorder from my past which the Lord never intended I should carry. This baggage had become sin to me, making me vulnerable to the Enemy, though still remaining hidden to me. I was becoming aware I was the victim of sin and baggage in my life that I did not know was there, but it was guiding my actions toward self-harm, making me sick and even more vulnerable as the years passed. Only when all this baggage had been exposed and fully cleansed could the Lord begin to deal with the reasons I had been so susceptible to it in the first place. Peter described this time as blowing the froth off the beer!

One of the hardest things the Lord asked of me was to cut my ties with my church. The reasons were clear to me – most of those at the church knew me as 'Sue who had the

breakdown' and all they could see was that I appeared to be having another one. I had been on the sick list for years. Very sadly I began to see that the congregation had become for me 'a poisoned pond', not because of the members, many of whom were dear friends, but rather because it had been the place for me of sickness and defeat. In choosing to leave behind old ways, old relationships, I had to make a temporary, though clean break with the past. It meant I had to resign from the leadership positions I still held. I felt even more vulnerable without the security of these crutches, but accepted my biggest battle was obedience to the Lord in my healing. I also began to see that I did not have the energy to explain and defend what the Lord had so clearly begun to do in my life. Much of what God was teaching me was contrary to what I had been taught before. Even I, in my desperate state, was having a hard time adjusting to these new ways of thinking, so I could quite understand how others felt.

For instance, I discovered that God was not at all pleased that I had studied the Bible intellectually, but did not let the Word touch my spirit. I had used my knowledge of God to help perpetuate self-deceit, by strengthening my mind in denial of my spiritual and emotional personhood. Because of this, for several months during those early days of healing, I hardly read Scripture at all. This felt like heresy to me. But old habits needed to die so that the Lord could teach me new ways. I also found that I knew nothing at all about the spiritual world. I did not really believe in the power of evil, even though I was to discover that it held me in so much bondage. The revelation of such truth meant I had to lay down my evangelical prejudices and risk allowing God to heal me in ways I didn't agree with! He seemed to touch all my 'hot spots', exposing my hypocrisy.

I can understand why many Christians do not like being healed this way. We demand instant healing. But for me

this was the only way left. If I had not proven faithful in these small things I could not have coped with the much bigger issues that still awaited me. God had to witness me making the right decisions, choosing life, before He could entrust me with deeper truth. In our Workshops we are able to provide a breadth of teaching that forms a foundation at the beginning of a person's journey. This is the fruit of many years in this work. But there is still no shortcut for faithful obedience to the Lord in allowing personal change in our thinking and ways of living.

Becoming The Person God Created You To Be

One way or another none of us are the people God intended us to be. Most of us are so selfish and self-centred that we see nothing in life beyond what we want. For our will is contaminated by our personal baggage and arrogant pride. As we see this pride, its sin and its toll on us, we will begin to 'fall apart' (e.g. lose this control). The resulting vulnerability allows God to show us even more of our sin – to crack us open like the alabaster jar. This is a Godly and ordained prelude to putting us back together – for He alone can bring wholeness to us. His intent for us, known to Him from the beginning of creation, is that we might worship Him by allowing Him to show us our sin and transform us into His Son's image. But most of us will need to fall apart before we know His wholeness putting us back together.

In each prayer session the feelings were released through pain in my body, both physical and emotional, as Jesus' light exposed years of suppressed emotion and lies. It was as if my body had become the repository of all this baggage. As the Holy Spirit stirred the feeling, the part of my body where it was 'stored' would respond. It was a shock to discover healing meant releasing the pain that I was carrying

in my body, before I was able to receive His promised wholeness. But I gradually, grudgingly persevered in obedience to the Lord and began to see that after releasing the pain, taking with it all the negative feelings, I could begin thanking the Lord for some freedom. When I touched the pain of rejection from a teacher at school and gave it to the Lord, it never came back. When I allowed the fear to flood me, or anger explode inside me, after the Lord took it it was gone for good. It felt like the stagnant stench of my past was being replaced by fresh air, even as the next wave of damage was being exposed. As I dealt with it properly, it went for ever.

One of the most significant areas which I had to change was my self-image. To say that God wanted me to love myself sounded like heresy. But I learnt that the amount of God's love I could receive and pass on was restricted to the amount that I could love the 'me' that God had created. If I could not love myself, I would be uncomfortable in the presence of any real love. I spent many hours struggling with God's requirement of self-acceptance. I had to choose to love myself. It was a decision of obedience, for there was not a lot of me that was very loveable at the time. But God had made me and He loved me. So who was I to tell Him He had got it wrong? This decision to love myself was to be the basis of many changes in my behaviour patterns and a decision I had to affirm repeatedly in the journey that followed. It had always been much easier for me to put the needs of others and the work of the Lord before my own needs. I began to discover that this was because, in the activity of serving others and the Lord, I could avoid myself.

Loving Oneself

Many Christians see love as a passive thing, where we let God love us. I have learnt it is in fact a deliberate act of our

personal will whereby we choose to love ourselves both for Him, ourselves and others. God may love us first, but we must respond in love to Him. This is a chosen way of life which we do to complete the circle of God loving us; we loving ourselves and then being able to love others who love God because of us. I have also had to learn that love is an emotional experience that involves our whole being. As we learn to love others we learn to love ourselves and vice versa. In trying to do this we will be shocked by how much we do not love ourselves and how this self-hate manifests itself in us.

I had totally repressed who I was and had spent my life trying to escape from myself. I had also cut myself off from people so that no-one could hurt me or find out the state I was really in. I began to see I knew nothing about myself, the person God created I should be. If I knew nothing about my true-self how could I *know* Jesus? It takes two to have a relationship, and I had been missing! I had no personal preferences, no likes and dislikes and I utterly despised my emotion. I had become the person I perceived others needed me to be. In my family I had grown up trying to take responsibility for my two younger sisters, denying my own childhood. In church I had taken up leadership in a passionate attempt to stay in control and thereby not be vulnerable to following others. As a consequence I had no personal life at all. I had no hobbies, no favourite food or favourite colours. My clothes were professional and bland and nothing about me was really feminine.

The Lord used the most ordinary of incidents to help me understand how much I hated myself. I was stunned to realise one day that the reason I tidied up the kitchen so fastidiously was so that no-one would know I had been there. I also found it intensely traumatic making a decision about what food to eat. And being at the meal table with

the Holmes family, to whom I was becoming vulnerable, was unbearable. The Holmes's enjoyed food!

The focal point of much of my 'undoing' was the meal table. For several months I found it exceptionally difficult to eat properly. I did not know at the time that my attitude to food was directly connected to my attitude to myself and to life. Food gives us life. If in our spirit we are not welcoming life, then food becomes a source of conflict. I did not enjoy food in the same way that I did not enjoy life. And yet the deeper the Lord cleansed my emotion the less I wanted to eat. The truth being revealed to me was profound. Just as instinctively as I had chosen not to love myself, I had also chosen not to live. I had made the decision unconsciously while I was still very young and it had been reinforced by a succession of choices and events throughout my life. I had chosen merely to exist, to fade into the wallpaper of life and do all I could to make myself invisible. In doing so I had rejected love and life, thereby rejecting myself. The Lord was waiting for me to reverse all these wrong decisions. I had to repent of the death I had chosen and begin instead welcoming life.

Life As Humility And Sonship

Although I did not realise it at first, life and death had become a very confusing subject to me. As a Christian I had read Calvary Road[1] and Humility[2] – the theology suited me and my baggage well. I must die! But the counterbalance of this, to live, was not so well received by me. I had known only death in my life, not life. I had to learn that God requires we all live a paradox. We must see ourselves as 'a worm and no man' by living in humility and brokenness,

---

1. *The Calvary Road*, Roy Hession, Alresford: CLC, 1988
2. *Humility*, Andrew Murray, London: Oliphants, 1961

knowing our sinful humanity. But we are also 'sons and daughters of God' and have divinity within our humanity. Maturity is being able to live at peace with both our personal daily death and life in His life.

I was astonished to discover within the first few weeks of living in Crescent Road that God was establishing a routine in my healing. Reliable patterns were emerging of how He wanted to work with me. Healing was a process, and the Lord had the agenda, the timing and complete control of the pace that would be set. He wanted to work systematically through the problems in my life in a carefully chosen order. In the past I had experienced very general 'blanket' prayer, covering a multitude of issues simultaneously. But the Lord was not content to work this way. Rather, He had chosen a slow, deliberate approach, waves of healing one layer after the next, that required my full participation at every stage. His healing in my life was to be characterised by systematic spiritual precision as each issue was brought to my notice.

Spiritual Surgery

The pattern of healing and change the Lord was using I now call spiritual surgery. I began to realise it was not enough just to see and feel the lies and feelings. Instead I had to find a way of specifically letting the Lord take them from me – it needed some surgery on His part. The preparation would start as I became disturbed by a memory, feeling or relationship. I frequently felt sympathetic pain in my body, so I would seek God's perspective on the issue – the diagnosis. When He revealed it, it was frequently the opposite to what I expected. This would begin the surgery itself as I let go of the feelings with repentance, giving the damage to the Lord. Holy Spirit cleansing followed.

> *Afterwards for a day or two I would feel exhausted, depressed and in shock. It was a natural reaction to the release from my spirit of the baggage and the accompanying trauma caused by the surgery – this was the time of 'post-operative' recovery. I did not need to fight or repress this condition and its feelings, just wait for it to end. Usually the next wave of healing would begin very quickly.*

Although I was committed to pursuing God's best for me, when it came to specific areas, I found myself struggling. I was shocked to discover that these negative behaviour patterns, though destructive to me, nevertheless felt like companions. I had lived with them for too long and had become dependent on them. The pain of rejection or the brittle anger had become a useful protection against risks of relationship. Did I really want to let them go? It frequently took several days after the diagnosis for me to focus on an issue and learn to hate it enough to want to get rid of it. My sin stuck tenaciously to me. I was learning the need to develop a righteous hate of the issue before I could separate myself from it in a session of surgery.

The sessions varied very much. Sometimes I did them alone, sometimes with Peter and Mary or with friends or folk from church. During the first three months of my healing I dealt with much of the deceit I was living in, like fear, self-destruction (hate), personal pain, bitterness, passivity, etc. To my shock I had to accept that if in my spirit I really liked the baggage, it would not leave even in Jesus' Name. Mid-session I frequently became lost in the confusion of lies as there was such a cacophony of noise in my head that I could no longer hear the voice of the Lord clearly. I found it hard to grasp the choices and shake off the damage in my life. My preparation was all-important. I was beginning to learn to hate what God hated – sin.

Many times as I tried to let go of an area of pain or a lie, it would feel as if it was attached to a hook, which held it in place. I learnt to recognise that if the damage was not spontaneously cleansed by the Lord as I touched the feelings, I needed to identify the hook that was still holding it in place. Perhaps it was a lie I believed, a choice I had made, or a deeper emotion I was unwilling to touch. I began to learn it was futile to repeatedly try to deal with an issue until I had found the hook. If it did not go, then the surgery had not been completed and I needed to know more about the diagnosis before trying again.

Frequently during these months I returned to the simple picture which Peter and Mary explained to me to describe what the Lord needed to accomplish. Like layers of an onion He wanted to work through one issue at a time in my life. He would expose the problem and peel off the layer in surgery, enabling me to cast it away and learn to live without it. Then He would expose and peel off the next, one sickness after another, one destructive attitude and behaviour pattern after the next until the baggage was gone and the person God created was free to grow. Only the Lord knew in what order He wanted to work and to what time frame. My part was to co-operate and respond to what He was doing. And of course, no-one peels an onion without tears!

At no point in the five year journey did I have an understanding of how far along I was. I would frequently think I had made it, but then be confronted by something more. I would many times feel there was so much more and yet instead would hear the Lord say that He wanted me to practice living with what He had given and not seek any more for the present. Persevering for so long was very tiring and many around me were critical of the on-going nature of the way the Lord was healing me. But Peter and Mary never failed to give me support and ministry when the Lord revealed a new layer. When I did not have the strength to persevere, their familiarity with the ways of God and with the Lord's relentless pursuit of healing on our behalf gave me the boldness to continue trusting and yielding to Him. I do not doubt that He released healing as quickly as my body, mind, emotion and spirit were able to possess it. Looking back I can see that the immensity of the mess I was in meant that it had to be unravelled in this manner. God's ways with all of us are totally unique and tailored precisely to who we are and who we will become.

3 *A Blockage*

It was Easter 1988 that I moved into Crescent Road to begin my journey into wholeness, coming back from the brink of a second nervous breakdown. During the following three months the Lord had dug deep into my spirit to bring to light many aspects of who I had become, all of which had been very well-hidden. But as He did so, I appeared to be getting increasingly sick. Much of the time I found it very difficult to sleep. I had started a new and more responsible NHS job just before meeting Peter and Mary. It was refreshing to be able to focus each day on departmental issues rather than the anguish of my personal life, but the gap between the competent manager that I was during the day and the turmoil of who I was outside work was getting worse. My professional and personal identities were becoming polarised. Without my 'masks' I lost all confidence in myself and felt totally unable to converse with anyone. All that I thought I was was being taken away, and I had nothing to replace it. I was facing the reality that in truth I had no friends, no hobbies, my relationship with the Lord had collapsed and even watching TV reduced me to trauma. I also found being in worship unbearable. I felt as if I was about to explode. Being at church invariably triggered a torrent of whatever suppressed emotion was being exposed at the time.

My relationship with my family was also changing, especially with my mother. I found some of the reasons for the strain in our relationship. Although it would be some time before the truth I was discovering about myself would bring a healthy reality in my attitude toward her. It was not an easy time for either of us, but it was to be the basis of genuine growth and healing.

The only person I felt safe around was Peter and Mary's son, Christopher, just turned ten years old. He seemed to be able to accept me whatever state I was in, coax me out of myself and even enjoy the stories I read to him. But there was no lasting relief for me. Many times I thought of looking for somewhere else to live, to escape the incessant exposure to truth in the Holmes household. But when it came to the crunch, I knew there was no other hope for me – I had tried it all before. And because of what had already been exposed I realised there was no turning back.

The actual prayer sessions were mainly releasing very intense emotion, sometimes accompanied by undoing the evil exploiting it. I had learned that evil is always eager to take advantage of wrong patterns in our lives and use them to gain a foothold. In most of the sessions the Holy Spirit easily and indistinguishably switched from inner healing (dealing with me) to breaking the power of evil, as He touched the various issues and removed the hooks. I would release the trauma of the lies, the anger, pain and wrong relationships and this would expose the evil authority hiding behind these festering feelings. I spent many hours in tears between sessions, pleading for the Lord to release me from the devastation that I was now beginning to see in my life.

Christians And The Demonic

Like most Christians I found offensive the idea that we can be oppressed by the Enemy, controlled by his followers. But I began to learn that this rather silly opinion on my part betrayed a profound misunderstanding of both myself, evil and the spiritual world. Just because I was converted, that did not guarantee Satan and his followers had automatically departed from my spiritual house. This fact was a shock to me, but explained much of my stubborn sickness. Hidden sin, though unknown to me, still required exposing and repenting of, before the Enemy's authority to remain and torment me through it would finally be broken. God is more eager than us to show us these vulnerable and unclean rooms of our house. I began to see that the baggage/sin and disorder in the rooms of my house created an 'open window' through which the Enemy could climb as he wished. But if I let Christ into that area of my life He would close the windows once and for all as He cleansed the room. We may not be able to stop the Enemy attacking us, but as we grow in deeper knowledge and confession of our personal selves and our sin, we reduce his authority to have a foothold and do us damage.

Whilst cleansing these emotions, the Lord was also dealing with my mind. It was essential that the two should happen simultaneously. He wanted to treat me with dignity and respect by showing me how I had got into such a mess. I must confess I was a most reluctant pupil, but there was no point in receiving healing if I was not able to keep the room clean afterwards. I needed to comprehend the truths the Lord was bringing and begin possessing and applying them. I had to know why I had been vulnerable to such a lifestyle to avoid doing it again. The Lord wanted to revolutionise my behaviour patterns and attitudes. Only when the healing had borne fruit in my transformed lifestyle would He be able to carry on with the next wave. I was learning so much that was radically new, touching so many feelings, that my ability to co-operate with the Lord gradually diminished. So He began applying the brakes for a breathing space and to prepare for the next phase of my healing. Instead of getting more understanding or toxic feelings each day, sometimes a whole week would go by without anything new happening.

I fought the Lord over this apparent delay. I was distraught. I felt in such a mess, so vulnerable. I was in a hurry for my healing, but Peter pointed out that God works in decades, not in days. The Lord was more concerned with doing it thoroughly than quickly. The following month we had a session of prayer facing what appeared to be a blockage put there by evil that manifested itself, but stubbornly refused to go. I knew of nothing in my heart to stand in the way of the healing. I was desperate to move on in the journey but the picture was of a shield being held in place which the Holy Spirit would not penetrate or remove. I had learnt that God and I were always a majority in healing, that nothing could stand in His way when I submitted to Him. And yet here was an obstruction which could not be moved… I did not understand the picture, but no more revelation came from the Lord. What was He doing? My emotional trauma was growing.

After a couple of weeks of this deadlock, Peter arranged for a special team from church to meet and pray with me. I took the day off work and prepared for what I thought would be a difficult session of prayer. Unusually I did not know what the issue was or the hook holding it in place. I was very frightened. After a few minutes of prayer, the team stopped. They all went into another room to talk. I had that sinking feeling there was to be no new freedom for me that afternoon. After about twenty minutes Peter came back and told me they could not continue. The team did accept that I needed more ministry, but could not go on because I was too fragile and sensitive. I should stop pursuing my healing for a time and just get on with life.

I was devastated. Angrily I struggled for several days to accept the word of the team as from the Lord and to submit to it. The following week Peter and Mary went abroad on holiday for three weeks. I was in a very 'undone' state. I felt utterly abandoned by God and everyone else. With a horrible sickness in my stomach I 'pulled myself together' to be a bridesmaid at my sister's wedding, playing my clarinet for the first time in nearly six months in the worship group at my old church. I felt such confusion and mocking from the Enemy. I was clearly still not fully healed – even after all this time and effort.

To make it even worse the Lord then took my work away from me. I began getting very sick and was diagnosed as having M.E. (myalgic encephalitis), a viral illness causing total exhaustion. It was very debilitating and lasted several months. I took leave from my job, slept a lot and had no energy at all. Gradually I realised that my apparent 'M.E.' was actually the Lord's way of giving me space to recover from His 'undoing' of me in the first stage of my healing. Without this total rest my recovery would have been much slower and the next stage of the healing delayed. The Lord 'maketh me to lie down'. Daily I cried out to the Lord, reminding Him not to forsake me.

I didn't understand at the time the meaning of the picture of the shield. But it turned out to be the diagnosis of God's next priority in my healing. From my childhood I had chosen to live in a private and exclusive world. I feared love, being manipulated or feeling vulnerable. I had sought, albeit unwittingly, to shut people out from my life because people caused me pain. The Lord had peeled away many layers in my healing to reach this point, but had now exposed this shield that I had put up around me. There was nothing demonic holding it in place. It was my own fear, pain and confusion as I instinctively began to defend myself against an invasion, albeit in this case an invasion I had invited from the Holy Spirit. I began to see that my whole life revolved around such defensive and controlling behaviour and the Lord knew it was impossible for me to change overnight. I had adopted a reflex, a script or 'safety' mechanism designed to block people from getting close to me.

The team had been right to stop. My shield shut out the Holy Spirit and my years of choices to construct the shield were the hooks holding it there. God would not intrude into my life against my will. I was desperate for healing but had to acknowledge first that the shield was in place and learn why I had put it there. Then I had both to choose not to defend myself any longer while also figuring out how to stop. He was requiring I change one of the most basic instincts of my life. He asked me to open my spirit, lower my defences and trust He would not abuse me. It had never occurred to me before that even as Christians we have the power to keep God out, whilst simultaneously crying for Him to come in and help us.

Sin Against Oneself

This was one of the most astounding lessons I was ever to learn. Much of our personal baggage is not actually what people do to us but what we subsequently do with that damage. For instance, a girl of nine is raped by her uncle and decides she can't trust those she loves. By the age of twenty-seven the fruit of that decision is that she is single, has never been in any long-term relationships and is facing a build-up of emotional illness that is pushing her to the edge. She realises that the original rape is only a few percent of the total damage she is now carrying. All this subsequent baggage is sin against herself – an attempt to compensate for the damage of the rape. Both in my own life and in the lives of hundreds since, this is by far the most common of problems. We are sick because we do these things to ourselves and we do these things to ourselves because we are sick. The Enemy feeds the spiral of self-hate and lies that proliferates the damage we do to ourselves. We are all so deceived about ourselves. Sin against oneself has proved to be one of the major sources of hidden deception and damage in the lives of those we minister to. It certainly was in my life. And we all deny we are doing it to ourselves.

Having been given such a miserable time by the Lord with my 'M.E.' sickness, I wanted to use the time to begin preparing myself for the next stage of healing, whatever that might be. Since I moved in to the Holmes's, Peter had been used consistently by the Lord to bring me words of knowledge or pictures as clues for the next issue. Now he said it was time for me to take the initiative in getting revelation from God myself. I needed to grow up and learn to listen to the Lord directly. He would help me interpret what I heard but I should expect no more. Even in twelve years of Christian life I had not begun to hear the voice of the Lord. So I started seeking God with a new desperation, needing to hear Him speak to me personally. This led to many hours of tears as I wept for the barrenness in my spiritual life. Peter made it look so easy. But he was right in requiring me to hear from the Lord for myself.

I began by learning the real world is the spiritual world. Everything in our world will have a spiritual dimension. I was dismayed to admit I knew nothing about this reality. This made me even more determined to pursue the fullness of my healing, for without such understanding I knew I would be crippled in my relationship with the Lord and my journey of healing.

So how does the Lord speak to us? By this time the Lord usually spoke to me in response to my specific questions. I discovered that when I found an issue to ask the Lord about, the answer would become clear in a few days. Perhaps the Holy Spirit would speak gently, so that I would gradually begin to 'understand' the answer. Or perhaps an unusual phrase would 'come to mind', which answered the question. Sometimes the Lord would just help me to realise

I was asking the wrong question! I also began to learn I did not need to wait for God to speak to me. I needed to learn to listen to what He was already saying.

Hearing The Voice Of God

When God has something important to say, He frequently whispers! That way, if we do not want to hear, we miss it. God does not want to intrude into our personal lives if in our pride we do not welcome Truth. I found the first thing He wanted to talk about was me. He wanted to show me areas of spiritual blindness and unrighteous personal inhibitions. Only after I was willing to deal with these to His satisfaction, did He consider it safe to begin telling me about spiritual truth relating to other people or what was going on in the spiritual reality around me. For the first time ever I began to see that God never stops talking! The Holy Spirit is saying more to us than we often can bear. He is more willing to tell us truth than we are able or willing to hear. Once I had learnt to hear (discern) the voice of God, it began to open a floodgate of conversation. The Lord wants our relationship with Him to grow from the occasional significant word for a special occasion, to one in which He tells us all manner of things, just because He wants to be our friend. God enjoys talking to us. The ability to hear God talking to and through me was the real beginning of my relationship with the Lord.

I was dismayed to discover that the very baggage I was seeking to be free from itself made it difficult to hear the Lord's voice. Often what He says gets twisted under the lies and deceit we believe. One of the reasons why God gives so much attention to our healing is that our past gets in His way when He is speaking to and through us. Without such healing we can frequently hear something said in our mind or spirit and passionately believe it is the voice of the Lord, when it is not. Other times, because what we hear does not fit our theology or hidden agendas, we attribute it to the Enemy. What we hear, from others as well as from the Lord, will always be filtered through our baggage and personal sin.

To circumvent the obstruction of my mind 'judging' His truth, the Lord often used dreams and pictures during my sleep to release truth to me and cleanse me. It is during our sleep that our mental control is least effective and this allows the Lord to release knowledge to us from both Himself and our own unconscious nature. Our dreams are often windows to self-knowing, provided we interpret them accurately. In such a way the Lord began cleansing me from the remaining fears and lies, often 'bad' dreams, which had been dislodged due to the surgery. Some were gone for ever, once they were remembered or touched by me. Others proved to be the beginning of a wave of healing as they exposed the secrets of my spirit.

One of the first issues the Lord showed me was that I was a victim. I had never realised before that other people's words and attitudes could damage me. The Lord reminded me of things I had heard and felt in my childhood and even while I was in the womb. A childish fear, mocking from my friends or betrayal by a teacher. None of it in itself was particularly awful, but when part of a much larger picture it compounded the damage. It all needed to be exposed and released. It frequently involved me letting out anger, both about what had been said and for the mistakes I had personally made. After finding the feelings, I had to choose to forgive, and as I did so the freedom would come. It was to be an ongoing process over many months and prove to be very hard work.

Being Hurt By Others Without Realising It

Having a spiritual dimension to our human make-up means there is a lot going on in and around us of which much of the time we will be unaware. People get angry with us. They are jealous, covet our friends or way of life, or do not want us to prosper. Or our parents wanted a boy and we are a girl! This can bring much personal confusion to us in our formative years and even later. The same is true of more overt physical and sexual abuse. Over the last ten years I have walked the road with hundreds of women who have had deep spiritual scars as a result of the damage laid on them by others. I have learnt that God is very eager to tell us about such ambushes and the subsequent damage we may be carrying as a consequence, if we give Him time to talk to us. After sin against ourselves, this is probably the second most common area of damage.

The other area I began learning about was that the spiritual world has order and structure, and that patterns of sin are often repeated from one generation to the next. I had begun to observe unnatural life and death patterns in both my father's and my mother's family. This gave me clues as to the roots of the problems in my own life. I had so far only sought the Lord for explanations of things I could see and feel. I began to learn about the presence of evil, to understand that personal choices for evil, even in our forbears, gave more authority for evil throughout the subsequent generations. And that all such choices produced consequences, many of which I had become the victim of through my own bloodline. The Lord continued to be very precise in His work in my life. The power of evil had also been very systematic and purposeful.

All this understanding was a little bewildering, making me nervous. In my own past I had never been personally involved in any evil activity, but there had been several pictures and words during the first phase of ministry which hinted at occult involvement in my bloodline. I had no direct knowledge of this myself. All the signs, however, were clear, especially the persistent pattern of premature death and prolonged serious illness through several generations, including my father's untimely death two years previously while still in his mid-fifties. The authority of the evil that had been exposed during the first part of my healing was given by my own wrong decisions and lifestyle. But this was something different. I had to respond somehow to the new knowledge I was now getting.

Bloodline Sin

The third and, thankfully, least common source of damage for all of us is that of bloodline sin. But when it is present, as in my life, its impact can be disproportionately devastating. It is also the most controversial. Scripture clearly teaches that we suffer the consequences of our forebears' sin (Exodus 20:5ff, 34:7; Lamentations 5:7, etc.), although we are not punished for it. It seems God has purposely made descendants accountable as a deterrent to parents sinning. The blessing to a thousand generations should make more impact than the cursing to three or four generations! Unknown to me the Enemy had a claim on my life that had become a significant source of damage. Some Christians have a hard time with such teaching, thinking it is unfair, but the exposure of this hidden sin was to save my life.

This understanding of the sources of damage in my life grew slowly over several months, particularly while I was sick with M.E. The increasing clarity about the damage (baggage) contributing to my sickness was exceptionally helpful. My expectation of God's 'stitching me together into Christ' was growing and as more sin was exposed so the need for my undoing became more obvious. I didn't want to stop until I had become the woman God created me to be.

My new-found ability to hear the voice of God gave me courage to pursue the relentless waves of healing. But then I had a shock. The Lord said I should go abroad. The realisation grew over a couple of weeks and was confirmed by Peter and Mary. I didn't understand at the time why I needed to go. It was very difficult, for by now I found it impossible to be around people and was still quite sick. I was struggling with many issues and suffering from frequent depression. The prospect of leaving the only people who understood me filled me with fear and it was only my second trip outside Europe, to a country I had never visited before. Worse than that, I had a real fear of the next stage of my healing. How could I leave when I was so undone? In gut-wrenching obedience I resigned from my job and made arrangements to travel to the USA. It was the obvious place to go. Mary is American and so had a lot of contacts and family. And if I needed more ministry perhaps I could visit the Vineyard Church in Los Angeles?

Just as I left for the States, nearly a year after first meeting Peter and Mary, the Lord exposed me to more feelings, again so well-buried I did not know they even existed. I began feeling an intense hatred of life, particularly new life. My nephew had just been born and I had the overwhelming feeling that I could kill 'it'. So much so that when I went to see my sister in hospital I didn't even dare hold the baby. This appalled me, but it was another clue from the Lord of the nature of the evil I was carrying in my spirit. These feelings confirmed other words and pictures I had begun receiving. My reaction was definitely 'abnormal' (!) and a clear sign to me that I needed to pursue hard the healing He was beginning to release.

4 *Breakthrough*

In trepidation I travelled to East Montana, where Peter and Mary had friends. The town was more like a village located in the middle of nowhere. Nothing ever happened in Circle. Apart from doing well in school basketball, I was their only other winter event that year! The anonymity I craved in my sickness in Bromley was no longer possible. I was catapulted into a farming community who were fascinated to meet me and loved my accent! Gradually I was dragged out of the shell into which I had withdrawn. I visited with folk, rested quite a lot and began to learn again to communicate to ordinary people on ordinary subjects.

But I was still sick and very depressed. Alone and isolated, crippled with fear about myself, my future, God, others… It was intensely difficult and for the first few weeks I struggled to understand how this could possibly be God's best for me. Apart from people, there was so little to do. I had to spend lots of time with myself, just being. I could not escape into activity or even into a comfortable home environment where I could relax. My instinct was to withdraw until my healing was complete and only afterwards learn to relate to people and participate in life. But the Lord was not permitting that. Healing in my spirit had to be implemented in day to day relationships and my personal change.

The Holy Spirit wanted to introduce me to more of myself and His means of doing so was to give me an empty diary, with a generous dose of social activity where I was the centre of attention. I never knew what would happen next;

being the subject of a joke in the pastor's sermon, invited out to the nearest pizza parlour an hour's drive away, or staying indoors alone all day staring out at the snow on the plains. I had to learn to give the Lord control of each day, each issue, each relationship. This spontaneous way of life became my daily prayer. The Lord's gentleness and sensitivity frequently amazed me. Gradually He was showing me how to dismantle the shield which had shut Him out.

In the midst of all this, my priority remained to concentrate on seeking the Lord. The church there had no experience of what I was grappling with. It was just me and God. I began reading the Bible again, meditating on John's Gospel, often just a verse a day. It was a real struggle to allow the Holy Spirit to use the written word to bring me the Living Word. I had so much to learn.

I found myself hearing a growing list of things He wanted to sort out. Some of it came through pictures, or sometimes a phrase or some new insight would release truth. It covered many areas of my life. Each impression, feeling, thought or reaction I would diligently write down in my journal. The phrases the Lord gave, mirroring my spirit, weren't pleasant – they were full of death and my hatred of life. I felt deeply entangled in the sin of my bloodline. It had become my own. God required I accept responsibility for my life and repent ever more deeply of the decisions I had made to live in darkness.

Repentance And Spiritual Knowledge

It was at this time that I began to learn how to repent. Often in our healing it is not enough to want to change, nor even to say sorry for areas of sin. We have to feel sorry and let that sorrow grow inside us in our spirit. If we are willing and persist the Lord will show us how He feels about the disorder and damage in our life. Seeing ourselves from

God's perspective always leads to heart-felt repentance – an essential stage in all spiritual surgery. To be effective, repentance should be affective.

Genuine repentance frequently leads to a knowledge of truth (2 Timothy 2:27). We often need to first repent for the sin that we know is there, even before we see it clearly. This process will offend our minds, engage our feelings and lead to the condition of heart that permits the Lord to entrust us with truth or knowledge that will then give meaning to our repentance and circumstance. We must be in an attitude of repentance often before we know what to say sorry for. When we get stuck repentance is always a good way out. Treat repentance like a muscle, give it some exercise!

Along with the death, there was a different set of issues the Lord began to expose. Again and again I saw myself shy away from people, their touch, their glance. I saw the split personality, the confident, professional exterior and the fearful, weak, 'people-phobic' feelings buried underneath. I saw my fear of my emotion and my fear of love. I recognised and confessed my despising of womanhood and I fought to accept that when the Lord made me a woman, He did not make a mistake! I began to understand that by seeking always to please others, I was avoiding the responsibility of being myself. I had been prostituting myself – the person God had created. I had moulded my character and my feelings on who others wanted me to be, listening to their voice rather than who I was or who God wanted me to be. In this way I had denied my true self to myself. I cried out to the Lord, pleading with Him to teach me how to lose control, to loose the tight grip I had on myself by opening myself to Him and others.

In all of these discoveries I kept repenting and seeking the Lord for breakthrough. I began to fast occasionally, when prompted by the Lord, usually just a meal or two, to affirm my desire for release in my spirit. Reluctantly I conceded that the Lord was building up a list, an agenda, teaching me what He wanted to change. This allowed me to begin to desire His ways rather than old ways. His intent was that there was a growing momentum towards life, so that even before a time of prayer I would already hate and be dissociating myself from the sin, ready for the surgery. Reaching this place prior to prayer is essential if we are to achieve in the time of prayer all the Lord is seeking to accomplish. We should not go into prayer blind.

I had plenty of opportunity to implement new decisions even before the baggage was gone. The lady I stayed with sold beauty products and insisted on teaching me to put on make-up. Never in my life had I worn make-up. I had hated even looking at myself in a mirror and certainly did not want to make myself look at all attractive or feminine. Everything I wore, my hair style, my actions, all these had been an expression of the choice I had made not to exist. As I was welcoming my womanhood in private, so Laura was teaching me to do the same on a more practical level. To start with I learnt scientifically, as any other way produced great conflict in my spirit. Later my willingness to wear make-up was to become a useful barometer of my personal progress.

After six weeks in Montana, I moved south to visit the Vineyard Christian Fellowship in Anaheim, California. I felt a rising expectancy. Surely here the Lord would release me from this sickness. For the first time in over a year I found I could be in the presence of God's anointing, without wanting to walk out in panic. I was able to participate actively in worship, a very encouraging improvement from my fragile state when I had left the UK. But I was aware the Lord was still restricting me to waiting on Him. In Montana the weather had been too cold to go out, in Anaheim it was too hot! So I continued to spend time listening. Again I fasted, sometimes for twenty-four hours, sometimes less. I also began an exercise programme, aware that physical fitness was a necessary part of preparing me for what the Lord wanted to accomplish.

The agenda was becoming clearer. Both lists that I had begun in Montana were now growing. But my choices were also getting clearer. This led to considerable pain and battling in my spirit. It was very obvious there was deep opposition within me to the choices I was making. That was hardly surprising, considering the enormity of the change after twenty-eight years of committed living in spiritual self-denial. I knew I would need help to find and possess the freedom to change. How was the Lord going to release this?

To my astonishment I found myself declining several offers of prayer, knowing it was not the Lord's timing. I discovered that as I found my spirit, I was more prepared to make decisions about my own life. Previously if anyone had offered to pray with me when I was in such need, even if I didn't want them to, I would have assumed they knew best and agreed. But for the first time I chose not to submit to folk in prayer when I did not *feel* it was right. I had waited eight months for this next session and knew it was going to be very important. I was also terrified! I chose to wait a little longer, rather than to acquiesce passively to any well-intentioned individual who might not realise the significance of the issues about to be exposed.

Trusting

I have met many women who have a very hard time trusting God. A great number of them feel the Lord has 'betrayed' them many times by not answering their cries. I had to learn to trust Him more than I was trusting others. For many of us this will often be the first issue in healing, to switch our allegiance to Him away from ourselves and others. But it

> often begins by our forgiving God for the past as we see it, and letting Him be a friend in our healing journey rather than continuing to be part of the problem. When you invite Him into a room of your spiritual house, you will discover He will sit on the floor and weep with you. He's on your side.

I continued going to the services, small groups and conferences. I began to choose to give my body to the Lord, forcing myself to raise my hands in worship, something I had never done before. I was able to stir my heart in worship and affirm with conviction my desire to be free from this baggage. In one of the services, I heard a phrase from the Lord as I was worshipping – 'a fortified city'. I froze with fear. Did it describe a place in my life where Jesus was not welcome? I invited the Lord to expose more, show me the root of its strength, so that it could be torn out and destroyed in any way He chose. Although I didn't tell anyone, that phrase began to disturb my spirit profoundly.

One Sunday about four weeks after arriving at Anaheim, one of the ministry teams suddenly had a free appointment the following day. They knew nothing about me and I had not even had the chance to talk with them and check them out, but I accepted their invitation. This was trusting the Lord in the extreme, but I felt it was time to do so.

Three people invited me into a small classroom. From the start I was terrified and couldn't answer their most basic questions – so much so that they spent the first half hour trying to work out whether I was a Christian. Inside I was fuming arrogantly – how could the Lord expose me to this? If they could not see I even knew Jesus, how were they going to be able to see the hooks with precision? But I heard the rebuke of the Lord. Was I going to trust Him to use them, or would I stay in control? In my spirit I submitted to the Lord and to them as His channel. And as I did so, they began to see what was happening.

They started to pray. This caught me off guard and in a frenzied fear I leapt from my chair and flew headlong into a wall! Thankfully I did not hurt myself. Gently but firmly they brought me back, sat me on the floor and called in a few more folk to join us. I had to struggle hard against the lies, the hate, the anger which was exploding inside me. Sometimes I could barely hear the team. Other times the words they spoke echoed intolerably in my head and heart. I had learned enough in previous sessions of prayer to know that I had to listen and co-operate with them and that I had to keep the Name of Jesus at the forefront of my mind and spirit, even when I could not do so with my lips.

There was much death that expressed itself during the session. As they prayed I felt its lure and for a time I was deceived by its attractive rest. My body became still as I was drawn into the lie. But in the previous months I had made my choice. I was choosing life and renouncing the death of the past. As the team repeatedly called on the Name of Jesus, I was able to join them and fight back against the death of my past, speaking out my choice of life. The Lord also exposed my hatred of life, the rejection I'd experienced at various times and the taunting in my spirit. Much of the battle was in my mind, which felt full of very aggressive and powerful lies. At several points the team asked me to repent of various decisions I had personally made, and to forgive those who had brought death to me. After approximately three and a half hours I ran out of energy and so did they. They stopped praying and encouraged me to rest. The session was over.

Alone in my room later that day I was too shattered even to cry. I felt intensely miserable. The stench of death was so strong. So much dirt had been thrown up. In my mind I knew that I had to rest, avoiding the temptation to evaluate during the next few days until the post-operative shock had begun to wear off. But that understanding did little to soften the sickening exhaustion in my body and spirit. Although I hadn't told the team, the Lord had brought to light the first half of the agenda He had been giving me over the past few months. The whole session had been focused around life and death and my willingness to affirm my choices made many times before to separate myself from my old way of life.

Being Healed But Feeling Wobbly

There is an assumption amongst many Christians that healing feels wonderful. But the day after open heart surgery a patient may perhaps feel even worse than before the operation. So it is with spiritual surgery. Even when ministry is 100% successful it still often leaves us exhausted. The deeper the issue is, the longer it takes for the spirit to recover and find a new equilibrium without the baggage. This is often accompanied by feelings of loss, anger, shame, etc. as the Holy Spirit cleanses the emotion and you see how evil the baggage really was. Feeling bad after such breakthrough should be expected, especially if the Holy Spirit is already preparing you for the next issue.

In the days that followed I rested but had no time for self-pity. The family I was staying with wanted to take me to Disneyland and out to the beach. Once again I was dragged out of my protective shell and forced to relate to others and live a little. But I was still very sore and bruised, physically and spiritually. I felt on an emotional roller-coaster, one minute rejoicing at the progress, the next humiliated and disgusted that it had been necessary. I turned to the Lord for comfort.

At the back of my mind was a nagging doubt as to whether we had actually finished the session. I said nothing to anyone other than the Lord. This time I needed no rebuke to remind me to trust the team. I would let the Lord tell them if there was any need to meet again. Sure enough as I was leaving church the following Sunday, the leader of the team came up and asked me how I felt. I was very embarrassed. It was the first time I had ever met him 'in my right mind'. I said I was recovering. He paused and then asked if I would be willing to meet with the team again the following day. With a twinkle in his eye he said that the Lord had promised a complete victory. That sounded exciting but also filled me with fear.

So a week after my first session, we met again. This time they were more prepared and had a team of seven, later increased to fourteen! They almost caught me as I flew across the room again when they started to pray. I had no clue of what they were going to do. But I did not need to know. The Lord had made it quite clear to them that they were dealing with bloodline sin and not just the consequences of my own choices. The Lord broke through in an almighty way, exposing and releasing me from many strongholds of death as well as much ancient witchcraft. The Lord had begun to deal with the hooks in my bloodline, exposing an evil authority I had unwittingly inherited through my family as the eldest child and daughter.

It was quite an intensive session. I did not have so many hard choices to make, for the baggage being exposed was nothing I had ever personally chosen. But it felt very strange to be touching waves of sickness that were older than I was. The pictures and knowledge were related to woods and occult practices, all very vague to me. Yet I could feel them in my body and spirit. The pictures being exposed matched dreams and words I had had during the previous few months. The team brought me to the altar of God and suddenly I saw an evil altar. The Lord brought to light bestiality, child sacrifice, massacre, and the abuse of love and sex. There was a lot of death, isolation, silence, adultery etc.

Again and again the Lord revealed this filth and the team prayed with me until I was able to choose Jesus on each issue and let go of the sin. There was little clarity and precision, more like working through dense jungle undergrowth than felling trees and clearing ground!

After three hours we were beginning to tire. The team asked me if I wanted to stop, but I was committed to seeing the breakthrough the Lord had promised. So the team leader left for a coffee (!), while we continued. We then confronted a blockage, a final obstruction. I was getting discouraged. Would the Lord fail? The leader came back into the room. Even before he approached I could feel the authority he carried. He said he had seen a castle which the Lord wanted to tear down. Then I knew – this was the 'fortified city' the Lord had shown me several weeks before. As he spoke I became engulfed in defiant rage and panic. The evil was exposed. The battle was won. For the next hour it felt as if the holy wrath of God burned through the fortress as the Lord destroyed it. All the envoys from the castle of darkness were destroyed. We saw (and felt!) the ground open up and swallow it. Jesus' victory had been released. The team had never come up against such issues before – but that didn't stop the Lord from winning.

This time when the session ended, although even more bruised and exhausted, I was exhilarated. All those who had supported me rejoiced with me. What the Lord had promised had been given. A network of evil over my life had been brought under the blood of Christ and removed. When exposed in Jesus' Name and the 'patient' does not want it, it cannot remain. What a power-full victory Jesus won on the Cross. He had been marvellously in control of both the sessions. I felt a whole dark side of my nature had been taken from me.

My move away from England and all the 'pre-operative' preparation by the Holy Spirit over the previous eight months had been effective. The hooks which were too comfortable in home territory had been exposed in the USA. The 'spiritual undergrowth' was clear and the source of the ever-worsening sickness in my life had been exposed and removed. I knew there was more to go, although I did not realise how much. But the Lord had cut through the next layer of the onion and my healing could continue.

In our ministry as we practise it today I am pleased to say these two sessions would not have been necessary. We have learnt and now teach people to co-operate with the Holy Spirit in cleansing little by little, step by step, to engage and release the trauma and pain of their past, however evil, rather than collecting up a list and trying to do it all at once! The significance of the freedom when it comes is no less and is easier to sustain than the more dramatic approach.

The exhilaration gave way to confusion as the shock and trauma of the spiritual surgery began to take its toll. But in faith several days later at a small Vineyard celebration I testified to the work of the Lord in my life, to His patience and perseverance through such an amazing journey. It was the first time that most of those who had prayed with me realised that they had been used by the Lord in part of a healing journey which had already taken fifteen months.

Around the time of that second prayer session, the family offering me hospitality could do so no longer. Within a week I had to move on. I wanted to stay around those the Lord had used to bring me such release, but the Lord had other ideas. Much to my surprise the evening before I left the Lord arranged a very different session of ministry at the end of a kinship (housegroup) meeting. I tried to prevent it happening because I felt so fragile, but when it became clear to me that the Lord had arranged it, I co-operated. In contrast to the other two sessions it was very gentle, very quiet, none of the same people and none of the same issues.

There was only one issue – me opening my spirit to receive love. The Holy Spirit touched me as I sought to open my heart. That exposed a blockage which was shifted in some ten minutes of tears of repentance and forgiveness. Again the Holy Spirit invited me to open my heart to His love and He exposed another obstacle. Relationships where trust had been broken, fear of being touched by love, preferring the 'safety' of isolation, painful betrayal... at 2am we drew the session to a close and my heart was radiant.

For the first time in my life I knew love and could feel freedom. Sadly we also recognised that we had not broken through all the obstacles. The freedom could not be sustained, because there were still issues in my life that needed to be cleansed. I knew those issues were the second half of the list, those relating more to my personality problems. But the Lord had not revealed any of these issues to the folk in Anaheim. I had to trust Him. That evening was a foretaste from the Holy Spirit of freedom and life that was to come following completion of my journey into wholeness. And it was affirmation to me that the Lord wanted me to persevere. Several of those who prayed with me that night testified that they had never before witnessed such a remarkable transformation during a session of prayer. The 'shield' I had put up, which had kept the Lord out, had also kept my spirit dry and withered. Now it was gone the Holy Spirit could begin to give me life.

Foretaste Of Healing

I knew after the third and final session in Anaheim that in my spirit I carried the healing with me. But it was too soon for that healing to filter through the bruising to change my feelings and behaviour patterns. The foretaste was not mine to keep. When we are undergoing extensive ministry we are easily discouraged and are very vulnerable. We may have

> *successful prayer but be unable to hold onto the benefit. What is released in our spirit in a few hours can take weeks and even months to permeate our daily life. But the Lord will often give a promise, a foretaste or a knowing for us to cling on to in the hard times.*

Almost until the time I got to the station for the thirty hour train journey back to Montana, I fully expected the Lord to allow me to stay in Anaheim. Surely I could grow a little more before moving on? But no. Yet again the Lord was not allowing me security in anything other than Him. Exhausted and disorientated, I returned to the friends I had made in Montana five weeks earlier. They were delighted to see me and in the week I was there I passed my driving test, went horse-riding and did a 360deg roll in a small two seater crop sprayer plane with a farmer. Then my visa expired and I found I was sad to leave – healing indeed.

I planned to travel across the border to Vancouver, renew my visa and then return to Anaheim, so that other issues could be dealt with after I had recovered a little. I had contacted the Vineyard fellowship in Vancouver who had arranged some hospitality for me. I naively explained to my hosts that I was just passing through while arranging my travel documents. I'm sure the Lord was smiling – I could not even guess what His purpose and time frame was.

I'd spent most of the first day in prayer in my room, beginning to sense an urgency from the Lord. But this time the focus of my prayer was not myself but the Church, the Bride, being readied to display the salvation of Christ in the last days. I also considered my future, where I would go on my return to the USA. I shared my testimony at a house-group in the evening. One of the group said they would like to pray for me, as they had a word from the Lord. I told them that was fine, because there was nothing on the surface that

I was feeling. It was one of the few times that the Lord totally ambushed me. The word turned out to be about insanity and I felt it straight away. For eight months I had been waiting for the Lord and now I felt He needed to slow down!

The following day I was startled to realise that the Lord had begun working on the second half of the agenda He had given me whilst in Montana and Anaheim. These were not problems of attitudes such as life and death or witchcraft from previous generations. This part of the list was to do with me, my personhood and personality. It felt even more intimate. I had a lot of uncertainty, doubt, discomfort and agitation. In a rather mixed metaphor I recorded at the time, the Lord had removed a layer of the onion to expose a can of worms! This new Vineyard team wanted to pray for me – but I was about to leave again. What to do? Daily I sought the strength to trust the Lord, leaving the control of my next few weeks in His hands.

Within a week, my visa application had been refused on a technicality. I was now stuck in Vancouver until I either decided to return to London, or found somewhere else to go. Unbeknown to me, the man who had received the word from the Lord for me the previous week had already fixed up a session of prayer. He knew the Lord desired to bring me further release while I was in Vancouver. I did not feel at all ready, but could see the Lord had brought it about, so after a struggle I submitted. The day after discovering I was grounded in Canada for a while, we prayed again.

This time it was very different, not physically demanding but requiring intense concentration and courage. These were issues I was even more frightened of touching. As the team prayed with me the Holy Spirit began exposing various wrong feelings I had about myself together with unrighteous attitudes I had adopted. The Lord replaced with His beauty the ugliness, shame and humiliation I felt. The lies of unworthiness and inferiority, the practice of habitual self-defence, timidity and fear, restlessness – these were all brought under the blood of Christ and taken by Him. Many were thoughts and feelings I had grown up with, but I had buried them when I committed my life to Christ, trying to become with my own efforts the new creation I thought I should be. But they had remained repressed in my spirit, driving me as an unrighteous hidden agenda. The Lord knew He could not give me wholeness without exposing and removing these hidden scripts.

Scripts

From our earliest childhood we all learn from experiences, relationships and situations. As we grow up we normally forget the details of these experiences but continue to retain our interpretation and conclusions from these events. These personal judgements we take with us into our future. Even by the time we are starting school our perception of ourselves and others has been framed by these scripts that are increasingly guiding our lives. Though hidden they are tramlines within which we live. We never stop writing scripts until we know better. But much of this learning can be healthy. Like not having to relearn every time how to make a cup of tea or drive a car! But if in our scripts we have experienced pain, rejection, self-hate, trauma etc., these will also be incorporated into our lives and become hidden agendas. They become a part of who we are which much of the time God never intended we be. For instance, our running from love because it hurt in the past, or hating ourselves because we were abused by hate and now believe this is all we deserve… Many of these negative scripts become subliminal drives influencing our daily reactions to almost everything. Often they add energy to our reactions way beyond what the situation deserves. But few of these scripts are part of our true self and our wholeness requires they be exposed and dismantled.

However, as the session progressed I became very agitated, not being able to clearly distinguish between truth and lies, between the declarations of who I was in Christ and the deafening accusations of my old way of life. Much of the ministry appeared to go in circles and after several hours we called a halt. We all agreed we had not seen the breakthrough we needed. I had been unable to separate myself from the evil voices and lies and choose the Lord. Later I began to see that part of the problem was a 'spiritual schizophrenia'. I was actually choosing to hide myself, seeking instead to become who others wanted me to be. We needed specific knowledge – a key from the Lord as to how to break this cycle and remove the hooks.

My behaviour was apparently so unbalanced during the session and the following days that some of the team wanted to send me to a psychiatrist. This really upset me. The prayer had touched something in my spirit which I knew had a deep root. I had allowed it to become exposed and now it was on the surface and expressing daily due to my intense fear of people and my traumatised state. It seemed as if I was again touching the sickness I had felt just before leaving England. But this time I no longer had the resources to control and hide it. In exhaustion and brokenness I declared to the Lord I would submit to psychiatric treatment if this was what He wanted. But my affirmation of trust and submission was all He required. Dr John White, a pastor of a neighbouring Vineyard and himself a psychiatrist concurred that the symptoms I was experiencing were evil and gave us the go-ahead to continue pursuing the Lord in prayer.

Knowing I was 'trapped' in Canada, Peter and Mary rang from England to say there was a job for me in Switzerland if I wanted it. But they made it clear I should not leave Vancouver until the Lord had completed what was on His agenda. I felt very unsettled and very weak. How could there be such despair two weeks after leaving Anaheim? The Lord was not revealing anything more to me, although I spent many hours each day in prayer and meditation. I began to fast, first for twenty-four hours, then longer. I heard that the folk praying with me would meet me in six days time and that I should prepare myself. They did not know what the key was to unlock the problem and we needed it before we prayed. They had thrown down the gauntlet to me, the Lord and the Enemy.

I decided to continue my fast and to dedicate myself to seeking the Lord for the revelation we needed. For five days there was no breakthrough. I heard much through the Word, through devotional reading, through dreams and in prayer. I saw a few things from the past that I needed to forgive others for. But I did not see the key. Only on the day before we were to pray did the Lord begin releasing it. Again a little phrase – 'a walking apology'. I got a glimpse of myself through God's eyes. All my life I'd seen myself as a nuisance to everyone – I'd spent my life apologising for my very existence. The revelation was simple and obvious, but there were shock-waves beginning to course through my spirit. On my knees I wept bitterly in repentance at the implications of this new knowledge. It exposed every area of my life, all my relationships, touching all my memories. I knew this was the key that would release healing the following day.

The next day the Lord provided another key – my new name. I clearly remembered how, whilst in school, I had adopted the name 'Sue'. Although I hated it, I took it because it was the name everyone else wanted to call me. I recalled the French lesson when I crossed my name out on all my exercise books and began practising signing myself Sue. I had given myself away to others. The Lord told me that He had given me the name 'Susan' and that was the name we should use in the session. I realised when we used the name 'Sue', as we had in the previous session, it gave authority for the old me to respond, since this name was rooted in my personal self-hate. Now I was to choose, in faith, to become Susan – the person the Lord had created me to be – leaving behind the old Sue and her 'friends' and lifestyle.

When we came to pray that evening I was very weak physically. But spiritually I felt much stronger, although full of fear. I gave the team the two keys God had revealed to me. They agreed and we began. I repented for discarding the person God had made me, and for living in self-denial. I chose to become Susan. In doing so I took away the authority of the Enemy to continue exploiting my wrong choices. I was choosing to possess the Lord's plan for my life, coming under His protection. Waves of sin were exposed as the Holy Spirit touched various parts of my personhood. The Lord cleansed me from the abuses in my life, self-abuse, drug and emotional abuse. He released me from the 'apologetic spirit' which had caused me to live in fear, the root of so many of my phobias. The hardest wave was associated with the manipulation and control which I had unwittingly adopted to defend myself. That one was quite a battle, but as I chose Christ and His ways, so its authority was washed away in the blood of Jesus. Four hours later I had received my new name, Susan, rejecting everything unclean that was associated with Sue.

The Deceit Of Control

Most of us have been hurt by others in the past, so we pick up control as a self-defence. But to my horror I began to see that any part of our lives that we try to control ourselves is outside the Lord's protection and open for the Enemy to exploit and attack. I had to learn we do not need to fight or manipulate to stay in control. Instead He has called us to give Him control as we choose to rest in His sovereign authority, trusting ourselves to His protection in every relationship. Often behind our need to control are lies like 'God cannot be trusted' and 'we can do better ourselves'. And in these lies is our pride, which blinds us to the truth of the way we are living. Laying down control in our spirit and welcoming His pure Life is a daily, hourly choice for most women. It often feels like a 'breaking' and is a battle that exposes many more areas of sin.

That night, like other nights following ministry, I was unsettled and slept very little. But after two days – much more quickly than usual – I noticed real release and change in my spirit and behaviour. There were a vast number of areas in my life where I began to taste freedom for the first time. Even in things as ordinary as driving I saw that while oppressed by my apologetic spirit I had been full of fear and a hazard on the roads. I had been more concerned to get out of the way of others than drive safely! And in possessing my new freedom I found my enjoyment of colour for the first time. When I moved in with Peter and Mary my casual clothing was as drab as my opinion about myself. Mary had begun to teach me what colours suited me and how to shop for them. But it was a strain for both of us, because of all the opposition in my spirit. Now for the first time I spent three hours in a shopping mall treating myself to an outfit of bright contrasting colours. I knew this was the Susan I wanted to become.

In the days that followed I had to reaffirm many times the decisions I had made in ministry, to leave behind old ways and choose to step out into this new freedom. Many little issues started emerging which I took straight to the Lord. I continued the cleansing in my personal times with the Lord as He tidied up many loose ends, the result of so much spiritual surgery in such a short time. I was well aware that my healing was a battle which I needed to treat seriously, not letting any area of sin or sickness remain untouched as the Lord exposed it.

I did not know at this time that the almighty work the Lord had done in my life in North America was merely the beginning of undoing the depth of the sin in my life. It had taken twelve months of preparation and six weeks of very intense ministry for the Lord to 'get a foot in the door' and begin to expose the deep devastation of my life. I was a lot more sick than even I realised. The exploitation by evil of my schizophrenic existence was being exposed and broken. But there still remained numerous very specific evil claims and curses on my life. The Lord, continuing my education, was shortly to begin the most precise and delicate part of the spiritual surgery and this would finally bring me complete freedom. But first I needed to recover a little. My faith could not yet stretch to accept what the Lord still had to reveal to me. How gracious of the Lord to show me the road only one step at a time.

5 *Recovery And Release*

I had agreed to work at an hotel in Switzerland in a voluntary capacity for a while, helping out the manager who did not have an assistant. But before I went, I flew via London to spend two days with the Holmes. In the time I was there, my feet never really touched the ground. Five months after leaving so sick, aware of extensive healing I desperately needed, I returned with so much that was new I could barely comprehend it. Meeting me at the airport, Christopher did not recognise me. He had never seen me with make-up, colourful clothes and a confident hope in my spirit. I felt like a child showing off a new dress! What would they think of Susan?

I discovered that the Lord had given them some encouragement for me, which Peter passed on as we all knelt together and thanked Him for His Sovereign work in my life. The Lord gave me a prophetic promise about my future relationship with Him. He said that if I kept my eyes only on Him and did not get distracted from the road He was calling me to, that road would lead to the foot of His throne in the intimacy of His presence. He affirmed that I now had the resources I needed to continue standing with Him at the centre of His purposes. But He also gave a caution – I did not yet *know* Him. The Lord challenged me to spend an hour a day on my knees, meditating on Him. I wasn't to pray or ask for anything, nor was I to read the Word, just meditate on Christ in worship, opening my spirit to the voice of the Holy Spirit.

My response to these words was one of awe and excitement. In fifteen months of healing I had seen my so-called 'relationship' with the Lord get thoroughly dismantled. All of my healing had focused on me. It was necessary, of course, because in my Christian life to that point the real Susan had hardly existed. The Lord was not content with such a one-sided relationship. Now that I had begun welcoming the person God had created me to be, I was ready to begin knowing the Lord. It was my heart-felt desire to be faithful in all that the Lord had given me and begin a relationship with Him in life and not death. But I realised I still had a lot of recovering to do. I felt steam-rollered by all the ministry I had received in the previous six weeks, very empty and uncertain. I was new, but who was I?

I was assured by Peter that the birthing of this intimacy with Christ would happen whilst I was busy doing other things – working! The advice proved right. I was very vulnerable, unsettled, self-aware. But at the hotel the hectic activity of a 6.30am – 10pm shift, with a couple of hours off after lunch, six days a week meant I had a lot on which to concentrate. Much of the work was very routine, although physically demanding – making beds, cleaning bathrooms, clearing tables. I learnt some of the principles of hotel management and enjoyed improving my German. But I felt permanently exhausted and in contrast to previous months had no time at all to wait on the Lord, save an hour I took each morning.

For several months of long hours and hard work, I sought to allow the Lord to establish the freedom He had given. I made it a priority to be obedient to the word spoken in my short visit to England, even though this meant getting up at 5am. However, the Lord had not simply filled my days. He had brought me to a majestic environment of startling beauty, in a family-run business in which His Name was honoured and which hosted His family. The hotel nestled on a hillside, overlooking the small fishing village of Iseltwald, on the edge of a lake near Interlaken, surrounded by snow-capped mountains. Kneeling by the window each morning for an hour, I enjoyed the awesome splendour of the view, matched by the stillness across the lake – no noise, no movement, no human intervention. It was a fitting backdrop to my meditation on the Lord, His nature and His beauty.

In spite of this, I struggled with darkness and depression during the first few weeks and felt exceptionally disorientated. The victories in Anaheim and Vancouver felt so far away. The magnitude of the spiritual surgery which I had received in the previous month had been vast and had shaken me to the core of my being. A caution from Peter began to echo in my mind; 'Do not under-estimate the impact of the recent ministry you have had. Give yourself space and time to heal.' The shock and trauma was being released gradually from my body, emotion, mind and spirit. I experienced a lot of uncertainty and confusion. I had a period of unusual physical illness, with my wrist in a cast, my foot infected and my other arm seriously swollen from an allergic reaction to a bee sting, all simultaneously!! They healed after three weeks or so and I began to see them as part of the cleansing process of post-operative recovery, although I did not fully understand this at the time.

I was frequently very discouraged. My fight to change old habits exhausted me, and why such sickness if I was healed? Relationships with the staff were also difficult – I felt vulnerable and did not want folk trampling all over me. The Lord knew I needed a hectic schedule which was physically demanding, with just a little time to look at Him and none to look at me. But the healing was taking place so slowly I refused to accept it was the thorough pace He had chosen. Many times I despaired that the healing hadn't worked. Where was its fruit? But God's cleansing in my spirit continued even though my mind refused to acknowledge it. The hotel was a safe environment, with no spiritual demands on my life. It was neutral territory which the Lord had carefully prepared, not only to allow me to recover but to keep me safe before He exposed more evil authorities which proved far more dangerous to me than anything He had yet brought to the surface.

After a couple of months I travelled to England for a week to help Peter and Mary move home. I met up with some of my family for the first time since leaving for the USA. They had no idea what was going on in my life but were pleased I had a job in Switzerland. I discovered that the previous month my sister had made a recommitment of her life to the Lord after at least eight years of spiritual wandering. In the aftermath of Jesus' victory over some of the evil authorities in my family line my sister had herself been able to hear the call of the Holy Spirit and choose more life. The freedom Jesus had won for me was extending through my family, even though none of them knew what had happened.

Families And Our Healing

Scripture has much to say about relationships and God's perspective on them in a spiritual context. Because we are spiritual creatures everything we do has a spiritual dimension to it and when we come to Christ this gives God a way into the spiritual network of our family. Over the years I have worked with many couples who initially come to us seeking help for their children. Our challenge to them is always the same – to sort out their own spiritual baggage. That will give their family, particularly children, a greater choice to let go of the same baggage themselves. We refuse to see that what we carry we also require our descendants to carry. Typical of this 'bloodline' baggage is hate, arrogance, fear and a low self-image. As we faithfully deal with this sin and disorder in our own lives our families can then choose to follow in our slipstream. Frequently we have seen children also choose to let it go and be restored to the Lord.

This time when I met Peter and Mary it was in shame. I felt I had failed the Lord while in Switzerland. I had a growing fear of talking to Peter again and was shocked to notice that for the first time in three months the Lord was bringing new issues to the surface. In a remarkable way, as we chatted the Lord began to reveal the next layer of the surgery which He wanted me to prepare for. I found myself suddenly feeling very cold and 'reliving' an experience which had never happened to me. It was very specific, very precise. Although it was disgusting, it was remarkable Holy Spirit revelation. Thankfully God does not only restrict Himself to talking to us about good things! The revelation proved to be the key, releasing knowledge about the hold of the Enemy over my life.

The picture grew gradually, but became very clear. I needed a lot of encouragement, as I felt an increasing horror at what I was seeing. To my amazement, Peter also 'saw' the picture. As the revelation continued, I would see one detail and he would add the next. Then I would see the consequence and he would describe yet a further detail. Never before had I experienced that method of the Lord releasing knowledge. But it was very vivid, and so remarkably supernatural that it effectively brought the incident 'to life'. In the months to follow I had no cause whatsoever to question its reality.

It began with feelings of a cool breeze, a dark night, the sound of waves on the seashore, an open beach, but with bushes and shrubs nearby. There was a fire on the beach, huddled figures around it, dark, staring into the fire. They were a group of women, one was in anguish and torment. I could hear her cries being carried away in the wind. Another of the women was older, had authority, had pleasure in the event, was in control. 'My baby, my baby', cried the young woman. Others watching on, the baby was in the fire, being burned.

Then we saw movement from the bushes, a man watching, gloating, not visible to the women. The women moved away, gone, the wind died down, there was quiet. After a pause the man came out of hiding and walked over to the fire, to the remains of the baby. He stood over the embers, stirring them, enjoying them.

There was a second picture, woods nearby, tall, high. A procession, a lot of noise, many people. Leading to an open space within the woods, overhung by tall straight trees. People in a circle, watching, applauding. An altar. A woman lying on the stone slab, frozen in fear, being made ready. Men around. A man coming near – the man from the beach. A rape?

Phew! We stopped for a break. I'd only intended a chat to explore what the Lord might be wanting to reveal, but what He had exposed was most vile and shocked me to the core. As the Lord had built up these pictures, I could feel them in my body and was totally consumed by them. I identified very personally with the young woman, feeling her grief. And I could feel the fear of the woman about to be raped. As I recovered I was stunned, too stunned even to cry or respond.

The pictures had been clear. Both Peter and I agreed that it had occurred on the Welsh coastline. We even had a sense of the time in history – the late 1700s. I later realised the obvious connection: my father's family had originated in Wales. More recently, my mother's family had frequently travelled to the Welsh coast on holiday. It seemed Wales was in both my history and my blood. As the Lord subsequently revealed more knowledge to us about the pictures, we discovered even our initial impression of the timing was correct. It substantiated the remarkable precision with which the Holy Spirit is able to reveal detailed knowledge.

But before I could evaluate what I had seen, the Lord wanted to continue. I was back on the beach, but could not see the women or the man or the fire. I did not know what I could see. I was straining to *feel* it from the Lord. Peter asked me what colour it was. What a strange question. But before I could speak, I knew the colour. It was black, very rich, very thick deep black. As I told Peter what the colour was, he told me it was death, the death that was still over my life. Then again, another colour, green – representing the lie that Satan was my provider. Red, the shed blood of the child which had been the 'sweet' sacrifice to Satan giving him a false claim on my life and then white, a profaning of purity and priesthood resulting from the idol worship in the woods. And finally gold, the worship that Satan demanded from his followers and those that had been given to him. I felt it also represented the binding covenant over me, requiring blind allegiance in my spirit to Satan as my master. No wonder I had felt such conflict since being a Christian. Never before had I seen colours in the spiritual world, yet here the Lord was using them to release new knowledge.

By the end of the evening I was very disturbed. I had not begun to evaluate it with my mind. But I was excessively troubled in my spirit, because what I had felt had been so real, as though it had happened to me. We had simply spent the evening talking and listening, but when the Lord does the talking, there is a whole new dimension to the conversation!

Living With The Spiritual Dimension

These revelations opened up yet another dimension of spiritual reality to me. Things that have never happened to us physically can be experienced physically as if they are or were real. Because the Lord has access to our human spirit He does not need to restrict Himself to what our minds judge to be rational. Spiritual revelation will often offend our minds – if we are not careful we may arrogantly attribute it to the Enemy because it does not fit our theology or previous experience. Grudgingly I began to learn that by the limitations of our linear human understanding much of the spiritual world is in fact not intelligible to us. How necessary therefore for the Lord to use unconventional and supernatural ways to impart spiritual truth from His world. As an act of His grace, both here and many times since, the Lord used Peter to simultaneously confirm what He was revealing to me.

The next day we considered the meaning of the pictures and their significance. Why had the Lord revealed what was obviously very dark occult practice somewhere in my bloodline? Had this not all been dealt with when the 'fortified city' had been supernaturally burnt up in Anaheim? It would appear that the Lord thought not. Who was I to argue? Only later did I begin to understand that in Anaheim the perpetual choices of death, epitomised by the castle, had been brought to an end. However they were the 'small fry'. There were much stronger authorities in my life, present specifically as a result of words and curses passed on through the generations, dedicating my life to the Enemy. These needed the direct and deliberate attention of the Holy Spirit and specific surgical removal by the blood of Christ. But this could be done only after the spiritual undergrowth had been cleared. In Anaheim and Vancouver the

Lord had done the weeding, but now He was ready to tackle some firmly established roots.

This weekend in England became a training ground for me. I was learning how to effectively receive from the Lord the knowledge to defeat the authority and consequences of sin. I began to understand the significance of my willingness to spend one hour each day on my knees before the Lord. He could use it as an intensive preparation for this ministry which He had planned and scheduled, but not told me about! It was my first introduction to the idea that the authority of sin meant my life was not my own – not only my sin but also the sin of others. Suddenly what the Lord had released to me in Anaheim was put into perspective. That had been fairly anonymous, but these new revelations were far more personal. It involved me. It shed a new light on my journey of healing. On a good day it was a relief to know that the Lord had it all under His control. He was releasing healing in His Way, unpicking the web of bondage over and in me. On a bad day it was horrifying to think there was so much unpicking to do and still some serious issues to deal with. I found that having tasted a little life in the earlier weeks, it felt like the Lord was now asking me to give it all up and focus again on death. The contrast was stark so soon after my first taste of freedom.

I am pleased to say that in ministering to hundreds of women since my own healing I have met few, if any, who carried such extensive spiritual abuse, or needed to unpack it with the same depth and precision. Even where I have encountered significant occult activity in people's lives, in most cases the Lord has been able to break its power and remove the hooks as they repent, without requiring the depth of surgery I needed to experience. It is almost as though my own schooling from the Lord was necessarily prolonged and comprehensive in order to build the right foundation for my wider ministry to the church. Whatever knowledge and experience the Lord may entrust us with we can be sure we will need in due course.

On my return to Switzerland I had to stop my habit of kneeling before the Lord for an hour each day. In fact I deliberately gave little time to opening my spirit to the Lord. When I was in the presence of the Lord, I could feel the heat of the battle that was brewing and I found it very disturbing. The Lord was waiting to engage the battle but I was too weak, so He was biding His time. That meant I had to wait as well without provoking a fight. I was reeling from the vivid reality of what I had just discovered, but I had my hotel job to do. I maintained my work schedule and was able to take more responsibility because of my several months' experience. But my inner life was deep in turmoil once again. Much of the struggle was a direct expression of my severe spiritual and emotional exhaustion. The Lord did not seem to mind. Although I frequently got confused, He knew where I stood and was preparing to confront the sin in my life in a personal and direct way.

After a couple of months I heard the Lord give me permission to begin preparing for the next round of the battle. I did not know when it was to be, but there was a change in momentum. The Lord warned me that it was a narrow way ahead and I would need to tread carefully. I resolved to do so.

Over the next few weeks, in utter disgust, I began to get more familiar with the pictures and gain more insight into the strategy of evil in my life. I began having frequent dreams which felt like nightmares, but released understanding about the ways of the Evil One in my bloodline. The events in the dreams had occurred many generations ago, but it felt as if it was all happening to me. Though I had no capacity to receive any more, the knowledge kept coming. I asked the Lord to give me strength and courage, both of which felt decidedly lacking.

My focus shifted from waiting to warfare. It became increasingly difficult to separate myself in my spirit from the oppression, evil lies and influence of the past over me. I found myself opposing the Lord when He was breaking through to speak to me. I could feel the death in my spirit poisoning my body, rather than the heavenly life flowing through my veins. As I was able, I declared to the Lord Jesus that I wanted Him to come in power in the fight that awaited me. I knew it was going to be a fight. I could feel and see the audacious confidence of the sin. There were many times of despondency as I became overwhelmed by the vulgarity of the ever-present revelation of my forefathers' activities.

But I also found a new revelation of God's passion for purity. Never before had I understood the significance of the Old Testament passages about the Lord cleansing the land of defilement. These concepts were to become food to my spirit as I pondered God's intense hatred of any evil practice and of any land or people that remain contaminated by it. I had been contaminated, but rather than being burnt in the holy fire of God, Jesus was interceding for me and He was bearing for me the punishment for the evil in my life. I wanted nothing unclean or defiled to be part of my life. Through Scriptures in the Old Testament and through words and dreams, I came to understand that the sacrifice of a child in my bloodline had given the Enemy an enormous authority over me. In my fear and confusion I did not have the courage to admit consciously to myself that the 'man' in the bushes was Satan and that the sacrifice meant he had a claim on my life. The acceptance of that was still to come.

During these days I was meditating on 1 John. I affirmed in my stronger moments that I wanted the love of Christ to drive out the Enemy. I chose not to shield any evil which stood over my life demanding idolatrous worship. Rather I wanted to expose the evil and give it over to the Lord God Almighty to be burnt, along with all the evil plunder that rested in me.

Two weeks into this new preparation and nearing the end of the hotel season, Peter and Mary visited me at chalet Edelweiss whilst on a business trip to Switzerland and Germany. Together with a couple of friends from the hotel they agreed to pray for me. With only twenty-four hours notice and whilst I was working long shifts, with no time to discuss the ministry in advance or get ready, we met for prayer. I only knew that the Lord had shown Peter a number of steel bands around my body, which were inhibiting the release of spiritual gifting in me. I told Peter of my fear of the 'man' in the pictures.

Spiritual Body Language

Over the years the Lord has introduced me to the intimate connection between the various parts of our human make-up. Spiritual bondage is frequently experienced in a related physical way in the body, so physical disorder is often a clue to the root of a spiritual problem. When used in conjunction with Holy Spirit revelation, this simple principle can be a useful diagnostic tool for 'spiritual surgery'. During the course of my healing I had become used to reading the various pains in my body as clues from the Holy Spirit of what He was allowing to surface from my spirit. Some of the pain was quite severe in the build-up to ministry, but I never needed to go to a doctor. The cause of the pain was spiritual and it always eased after the spiritual surgery was completed. Frequently, once I had identified the spiritual hook through interpreting the 'body language' with the help of the Holy Spirit, the pain would ease until the time of the surgery itself. I was a novice at spiritual body language and frequently asked Peter to help me with the clues. But there was no better way to learn its significance than in my own life and it was proving invaluable experience.

That evening Peter introduced the work of the Lord in my life to the folk who were to pray with us. It was the first time they had done anything like this! As he taught the concept of 'spiritual body language' I saw the connection with the painful infections and injuries I had experienced on first arriving in Switzerland. The steel bands were pictures of the areas of my life in which the sin had some authority. The particular part of my body that each held in bondage was the clue about what damage the sin was creating. There was a steel band around my head which represented the discernment and knowledge which was prevented from being fully released in my life. There was also a collar around my neck, which was placed there to prevent me from using my voice to sing praises to the Lord. My wrists were in shackles, preventing me from freely lifting my hands and leading worship. And there were various steel bands around my stomach, womb and chest, representing the Enemy's claim on my womanhood and the impact of the sexual abuse in my bloodline.

Having recognised the Fatherhood of God, the Lordship of Christ and His salvation on the Cross, we welcomed the Holy Spirit to minister Christ amongst us that evening. We began by cutting through each of the bands around my body by the blood of Christ. I felt intense pain in that particular part of my body as each band was mentioned. In fact the pain usually occurred in advance of Peter declaring which area the Lord was going to touch next. I knew in my spirit and body before I knew in my mind what the Holy Spirit was doing.

I was surprised to find the Holy Spirit focusing on the area of my willingness to give life, both physically and spiritually. The Lord had been speaking to me very specifically about it in the previous six days. I had felt a growing awareness that my disgust of evil activity passed on through my bloodline meant I felt I did not want to have any children, ever. But the Holy Spirit had made it clear that this did not please the Lord. He wanted me to be willing to be a source of life, physically should I ever get married, as well as spiritually. I was not to hold any contempt or fear of new life – that was not of God and would lead to more sin. I had struggled with this for several days, but eventually declared my willingness to the Lord. My surprise in the session was that I had not told anyone of this and yet here the Holy Spirit was addressing the issue quite thoroughly through the team. It was another example of how the Holy Spirit had prepared me in great detail. I could not have moved forward and seen real breakthrough if I had stopped and discussed this one with the Lord mid-session before submitting to Him in my spirit.

So we moved on to another area of my body, my knees, symbolic of Lordship, 'bowing the knee'. It was the only area where I had a medically recognised weakness since my childhood, although no-one had been able to identify the cause. Suddenly I knew with a stunned shock that ricocheted through my body that we had come to the root of the evening's session. Clear as day, I saw the 'man' on the beach stirring the embers of the fire. No longer hiding in the bushes, not cowering but blatantly and calmly relishing the sacrifice. I could smell the fire and the burning. I became engulfed in the death and lost the ability to respond in my body to those who were praying with me. But it was only for two or three minutes – my spirit was stronger and less intimidated by the authority of death over my life.

So what should I do with this 'man'? In the precision of spiritual surgery, the Lord knows exactly how He needs to undo sickness and oppression from our lives. The team began to banish the 'man', to return him to where he had come from and cut him off from my life. But he did not go. The words were ineffective. It was not that he fought the words, just as if they did not apply to him. Then through revelation from the Lord, the team changed tack. They declared that the Cross of Jesus stood between the 'man' and I, that his words were erased by Christ and therefore they had no authority over me. Christ had taken my place. That provoked a reaction! There was a torrent of evil denunciation in my head that this was not true, effective or possible – a sure sign that the Lord had given us the key!

At this point I was struggling. I wanted the 'man' to go away. Why was he not going? Why could I still see him and feel him? The team began addressing me rather than being distracted by my reactions. They were bringing the word of the Lord to me. I had to turn away from this 'man' and look at the Cross. But part of me was captivated by the 'man's' presence and authority. I wanted him to leave and for me to see him go. Again the command from the Lord was that I had to look away, turn my back on the 'man' and look only at the Cross. It was intensely difficult, but in my spirit I submitted and responded to the Lord's command. In fear and desperation I focused on the Cross. It was very distressing – I could not see or feel the Cross. But I fought to keep looking away from the 'man', toward the Cross, in faith.

As I did so, Peter broke out into a tongue in English, the like of which I had never heard before and had only happened to him once or twice in his previous ministry. It was the only time throughout the entire journey of my healing that Christ spoke directly in the first person through one of the team. It had such tremendous authority and power. He spoke directly to the 'man', Satan, who was claiming my life as his own. It was the first time I was confronted with his cold calculating claim on my life – the authority of

Satan to possess me. Christ personally addressed Satan on my behalf. He challenged Satan as to who really owned me. Christ declared His prior claim on my life and that never again would I be in bondage to Satan's will or purpose. For a time I became the battle ground of a violent and eternal heavenly dispute between Christ and Satan. I did not need to participate or fight. This one was not my fight. Christ was taking it up personally on my behalf and in my stead. My part was simply to continue to look to the Cross. When I looked away at Satan, in fear and disobedient unbelief, I got in the way of my Lord's ability to defend me. But when I steadfastly looked at the Cross, clinging to Christ's death for me, it became the invitation to Christ to act for me. There was no debate. Christ's claim had more authority than Satan's. With a holy wrath which I felt in my body, the Holy Spirit took hold of the new ground which Christ had opened up for me. The team invited the holy purifying of Christ into my life. I began to retch, coughing up what felt like the foul and contaminated lining of my stomach. The Holy Spirit was applying the cleansing of the blood of Christ. Satan's claim over me was broken, even though he didn't go.

Christ And Satan

This encounter was the turning point in my healing. And from it I have continued learning lessons about Christ's work for me. It was clear to me that the Enemy answers directly to Christ. And that it can be a waste of time challenging the Enemy unless the Lord has first given us the knowledge of truth, to be able to counter his claims and specifically renounce them. Evil hides behind lies, half truths and our lack of understanding of Satan's ways and authority. Unless we are able to precisely state and expose the web of authority the Enemy has over the person, we may not actually be able to renounce and remove a specific claim.

> *Blanket prayers in the Name of Jesus may work but often just lead to a huge confusing turmoil of emotion and pain, sometimes going on for several hours and much of the time, if we are honest, ending in defeat. I have learned that for a clinically successful session with least harm to the person we should always ask by what authority the person is bound and only go ahead with the prayer when we know. The knowledge becomes our authority to act in Christ's Name. In our ministry today we always invite the person to themselves hear this knowledge from God in the first instance. This best prepares the person for the healing to come and gives us permission to stand with them. It is not for us to tell them.*

I was shattered. I crawled to bed for a very disturbed night's sleep. When I woke things seemed unclear. What had happened the previous evening? What had been achieved? It all felt very disjointed and I was appalled at the thought that Satan had not been cast out of the picture. I talked at some length with Peter and Mary. Through them I gained an understanding of what the Lord had and had not accomplished and the implications for my life. It was not what I wanted to hear. But it was real and represented profound spiritual truth.

They had been unable to banish Satan from the pictures, because God had not been able to. Satan had a two-fold right to be there. Firstly he had been invited into my life through the sacrifice of the baby in the earlier generations. Satan had become my 'lord'. Secondly God has given Satan permission to roam this earth for a limited time. Satan cannot be banished from it, which was in effect what we wanted to do, for 'his time has not yet come'. Satan is, temporarily, the prince of the air. We cannot yet send him to the pit. This will be Christ's triumphant task in the last days.

I had to accept that I would live my life knowing Satan had a claim over me, though it was inferior to that of Christ. The Enemy also has permission to be on the earth, permission from God. So how can I survive knowing this? Let me quote from my journal, written the following day; 'The "man" is behind me, trying to exercise control, to demand my life and manipulate it (demanding further sacrifice, taking my life as a living sacrifice until he chooses to end it). But the Cross is in front of me. And when I kneel in worship before the Cross, then the Enemy's demands go over my head, because I am bowed down. They are absorbed in the Cross. Jesus has taken my place and given Himself, His life for mine. The Enemy demands a life, Jesus gave His for me and then conquered death and rose again. In the blood of Jesus is my salvation.' Thank you Lord.

How powerful is the finished work of Christ when the Slain Lamb becomes the Warrior King and fights for us against Satan and his followers. My command from God and my hope for the future was and is to fix my eyes on the Cross and bow down before my Lord and Master Jesus Christ. That is my only safe place. When I step outside God's way, then I move into shadowy ground where I am again exposed to the Enemy and he rapidly attacks. My Enemy is driven out, but my deliverance must continue to be daily. Each day's salvation will be ample for the day, but I must remain at the Cross for my protection from the claims of the Enemy on my life.

6 *Introducing 'Inner Healing'*

In the midst of my traumatised, bewildered and exhausted state, life went on. The hotel was closing for the winter so a week later I returned to England after ten months travelling. So much had happened to me whilst I had been away. The Lord had been exceptionally faithful. I had left with a few clues of the extent of the damage in my bloodline. I returned knowing the Lord had exposed and over-ruled Satan's lordship in my life. When I departed, I had been unable even to hold a conversation with anyone. I was also too physically sick to be able to work full-time and found worship unbearable. By the time I returned to the UK I had successfully completed six months of very demanding hotel work in a multi-lingual setting and my relationship with the Lord had benefited from my early morning hour a day. I had been meeting with Jesus. I also found that many of my personal problems were being healed. I no longer felt the need to apologise for myself all the time. Even walking down Bromley High Street felt totally different, now being able to hold my head up and recognising my right to choose what I purchased, instead of permanently deferring to others out of fear. And of course, having begun welcoming my real self, Susan, I was now developing tastes, opinions and preferences on which to base my choices.

But in spite of my new freedom, the build-up to Christmas was miserable. I was waking from a nightmare. In my absence life had gone on for everyone else. But for me, I had no job, no home, no church, no friends. Like the Israelites, I had experienced a supernatural deliverance from slavery and yet the barren wilderness I found myself in was equally unbearable. I felt isolated, misunderstood and confused. What now?

Peter and Mary made no attempt to ease the pain of my reintegration into everyday life. Their challenge was quite simple. Although the Lord had finished His work of deliverance for the time being, there was a totally new, radically different and utterly essential work He was about to begin. Instead of my past, the focus of attention was to be me and my future in Christ. I may have been freed from slavery but I was still living as if I were a slave, with all the feelings and habit patterns that went with it. Would I continue to wander in the wilderness in this way or was I willing to battle to take possession of the 'promised land'? I was about to be introduced to the concept of the vital, life-releasing ministry of inner healing.

Possessing Healing

Before I met Peter and Mary the Lord had brought me some measure of healing but I had been unable to hold onto it. One of the reasons this happens is that we are either unaware of or unwilling to walk God's way in the fullness of our new-found freedom. I had always assumed that deliverance was the end – the final step of healing. Isn't that what happened in Jesus' ministry? But I discovered that deliverance, confronting the evil in us, was merely the clearing of the ground for the fullness of healing to begin. The real miracle in many of Christ's healings was not the sick being healed, but that they then ran, shouted, saw – using in wholeness that area of their body that had been damaged for many years. It took lots of practice, some of it painful, to learn to walk without a limp so late in life! Inner healing for me was the Holy Spirit's 'after-care', teaching me and allowing the Lord to release an abundant harvest in my life. Without adopting this approach, learning its hard lessons, much of the fruit from ministry would have been lost or stolen in my life. Without inner healing, confronting the evil in us can be in vain. Wholeness for us all is a life-long journey of discipleship, not a time of prayer, however dramatic it may be.

Peter explained that the spiritual surgery had given me the potential to live new ways. But in itself this was not the healing – just the first step. The slavery had left behind old habit patterns, attitudes, misunderstandings and memories of pain – what we now call *scripts* in our ministry. The Lord was now requiring I allow Him to clean out their unrighteous ways, filling me with His Holy Spirit. If I did not make these changes the persistent old practices, thoughts and feelings from the disorder and sin of my past would become their own invitation for the damage to take root again. We all have to learn to accept that we have a very important role to play in our journey into wholeness. It is not something God does to us where all we need to do is passively wait on Him. It requires our daily active striving for the wholeness He promises us all.

The Lord spoke to me through a familiar metaphor. My life was like an abandoned house, derelict, shabby, uncared for. Until recently the Enemy had a claim on the whole house but was now being driven from some of the rooms. The Holy Spirit was beginning to inhabit the house, cleaning it up with my help room by room, floor by floor. But most of the rooms were still empty and bore the scars of trespassers. I had to choose to go in, close the windows to the Enemy, and occupy all the rooms the Lord had opened up to me. Little by little I had to change and consciously co-operate with the Holy Spirit in doing so.

I deeply resented this next stage of my healing. The battle had been long enough. Why could I not just get on with living? I wanted to dump my past and start again. I was even more dismayed to discover that the key in this inner healing was welcoming my feelings – the same bouquet of feelings from my past.

I still despised my emotions. I had abused and suppressed them, managed and controlled them all my life. The idea of welcoming them felt very foreign. At the beginning of my journey of healing the Lord had started touching me through my feelings. But they were all negative and painful, related to my past. I could not conceive of allowing any emotion to be a regular part of healthy living. I didn't want my emotion and didn't see any use for it. Indeed I did not consider feelings to be an integral part of who I was. Instead I had isolated them – something detached from me. I was staggered to hear Peter tell me that my emotion, emanating from my human spirit, was who I really was. My feelings were a fundamental part of my being. And even more remarkably the Lord wanted to use them, first in this next stage of my healing and then as an ongoing part of my daily life.

Righteous And Unrighteous Emotion

We have all been brought up to believe in good and bad emotion, but I was about to learn there are no 'bad' emotions. As a church we have divided emotion into good and bad, even though from Scripture we can clearly see almost all emotion has both a righteous and unrighteous dimension. Scripture shows God expressing a lot of emotion that many of us would not usually welcome; anger, hate, jealousy, etc. So what makes emotion unrighteous? I had collected (and buried) a lot of emotional trauma from my past, most being painful emotion. My spirit was full of fear, hate, anger, shame, guilt, etc. I began to learn God never intended or required I carry these feelings. They had been toxically festering deep inside me for many years, spilling over into every area of my life. As I let go of this historic pain by engaging it, my emotion could be a more spontaneous expression of who I was becoming. I was no longer dragging the hurts of my past into my future. This process, and the growing sensitivity it brought to my restored emotion, became an increasingly key element in my maturing in Christ.

Peter introduced inner healing to me at a very practical level – the first step was that I had to learn to cry. My emotion was choking, overflowing from reservoirs of hurt which the Holy Spirit wanted to take. My tears were like fresh water being poured into a glass of oily waste, sinking to the bottom and pushing out the dirty oil above, cleansing and healing as they did so. So the Lord wanted to press through my emotion with my tears, exposing more of me that He could possess and anoint. The pre-requisite was my acceptance of myself and my emotion. I had to welcome my feelings, whatever they felt like and bring them to the Lord for Him to redeem. No tears go unnoticed by the Lord. He looks with compassion upon them and even collects them. I had to learn to release the years of suppressed pain, anger, fear and frustration through the simple medium of tears.

Initially the first two years of my healing felt easy in comparison to the daily struggle of inner healing. This new part of the journey was more gradual and demanded hour after hour of concentrated attention. The Holy Spirit stirred memories as well as using various situations as a trigger for the healing He was releasing. Nothing was too small for His attention and I found TV, shopping, cooking, reading, in fact every part of my life became a channel to help recover more of what had been stolen from my sick past. But what really astounded me was to find that after an hour of deep sobbing, the pain really did go – for ever. Sometimes I knew what the pain was and could associate it with specific relationships or events. Other times I would feel the pain and let it go without ever knowing what it related to. My mind was quite offended not to be kept fully informed of all these details, but I gradually learnt to trust the Holy Spirit's work in my spirit without needing to stay in intellectual control. I began to practise a 'need to know' policy – if I didn't need to know, God didn't need to tell me!

Over the following months the Holy Spirit touched a variety of very specific emotions which I was able to feel and release. The first was my shame. It was so intense. I'd known it in the womb when I'd felt my mother's confusion during her pregnancy and concluded I was the cause. I'd learnt to be ashamed of myself. And during my life it had become even more established, as I found numerous ordinary situations which I could not cope with. In Vancouver the hook attached to my shame had been removed. Now the Holy Spirit was releasing the pain related to this shame. After hours of tears, feeling the shame torment my body, the Holy Spirit took this shame and I felt clean. For the first time in my life I was no longer ashamed of who I was.

Then on to the next feeling – I felt completely without hope. How ridiculous, when the Lord had done such a vast work already and released so much to me. I knew I should have hope, I could conjure it up in faith, but in my spirit there was none. What I thought contradicted what I felt. What was the root of feelings of such hopelessness? Could it be from the womb, when I felt I was not loved or wanted? The Holy Spirit stirred up the 'memory' and I began to cry. Then having released all the suppressed pain, I could choose to receive the True Hope brought to me in the Holy Spirit. I meditated on Scriptures revealing our hope in Christ. This in turn brought more tears of cleansing... and even more hope. I saw hope being given to be as a gift, not hope I had to manufacture or strive for.

Sometimes the Holy Spirit not only released the feelings, but also taught me about them. Anger was a subject on which I needed much tutoring. In the passivity of my chosen lifestyle I had believed that anger was wrong, even evil. In fact I had convinced myself I didn't have any! My mother was proud of the fact that I was the only child she knew who had never had a temper tantrum. But I began to learn that in God's righteousness anger is a healthy God-given defence and warning mechanism. It was many months before I could begin to use anger this way, but I began by confessing my willingness to learn this lesson. I had an explosive backlog of anger that I had suppressed. Although always in private and never directed to the individual in person, it was essential that I released the anger from my life. It had remained dormant for far too long, turning toxic in me over the years. I was given permission from God, even commanded, to release the anger. I learnt how to do so for the first time in my life. I discovered that even the most volatile and traumatic anger will evaporate once confronted. I declared I did not want it any more and said sorry for carrying it for so many years. I gave it into the Cross.

But the cleansing of the anger bore little relationship to the volume. Years of pent-up anger would be released in a short time when I recognised it was there and was willing to engage it and let it out. There were many evenings I came before the Lord and the Holy Spirit exposed my anger related to a particular memory or relationship. When I touched anger the Holy Spirit was able to take it from me and bring healing. Along with tears the cathartic release of anger became the most frequent means of on-going cleansing and healing the Holy Spirit was using in my life.

But hand in hand with the anger, I had to learn about

forgiveness. And here I had a real struggle. I thought I had already forgiven, so why was I still angry? I was shocked to discover that my forgiving felt like condoning the sin, that those who had hurt me would 'get away with it' if I forgave. So I secretly held on to the anger, coveting a desire for revenge. The decision to forgive was merely an act of my will, burying deep inside me the real emotion.

Revenge

I had to be reminded frequently that true forgiveness does not condone sin. Rather, we voluntarily give over to God our right of revenge, for His just judgement of the person. Revenge is God's idea and He recognises we have the right to expect justice. But He asks us to hand it over to Him, so that we can be free from the pain of the abuse and betrayal as well. True forgiveness must always involve our voluntary act of giving over to God our right of revenge, in order for Him to judge the person in any way He sees fit. This allows us to let go of the person or events involved and to move unencumbered into our future without the all-consuming energy of the revenge.

I began to learn to forgive others not for their sake, but rather for my own benefit. I saw that without forgiveness I was still vulnerable to those who had done me damage, and the memory remained alive in my spirit. Their hurt and abuse was still clogging up my life. My unwillingness to forgive meant the Lord could not help me. The sin stood in the way. But also, the open wounds allowed others to hurt me, making me vulnerable, while permitting Satan to take full advantage of this damage. Once I had forgiven, laying down the revenge, the spiritual tie between me and the person who hurt me was finally broken. In Christ I could find protection both from them and from their intent. I began laying down the revenge, issue after issue, person after person, giving it to God. I was dismayed to find so much buried anger that had been choking my spirit – no wonder I had been so sick.

I also had to learn that anger was often merely a defensive mechanism to prevent people getting too close and prodding my pain. Letting go of the superficial anger allowed me to engage the deeper pain hiding below it. I learned that unless I was willing to give the accompanying revenge to the Lord, He was unable to take the pain. So for instance, the anger and hurt I discovered I carried against my mother when she refused to accompany me the first day of junior school all evaporated when I engaged it. But I discovered behind it a pocket of fear and isolation because my favourite teacher, Miss Williams(!) had left and got married. Likewise, when I repented of the revenge I felt towards a couple who betrayed me at church years before, the pain and shame entangled with the memory all left straightaway.

One very painful area of my family life that became the subject of the Holy Spirit's attention was my father. He had died before my journey of healing had begun, before I had started to find out who I was in Christ, to lower the shield that cut me off from all relationships. That had meant I hardly knew him. Suddenly I became overwhelmed with grief. There was so much I felt for him, so much I wanted to say to him. Before the Lord, I said sorry to my father for letting him down. It wasn't that I had actually failed him, I just felt as if I had. I had to release the feeling, for my cleansing. I felt angry with him for deserting me (so irrational!), angry with God for letting him die. Could I have saved him? The pain was so intense that it frequently felt as if he had died just the day before. The Holy Spirit exposed a lie that I had lived without even realising – I believed my father had not loved me. It was so deeply embedded in my spirit I did not realise it was there until the Lord brought it to light. But when I saw it, I was able to renounce it. It led to many tears and much more cleansing.

> ### Saying Good-Bye
>
> *Scripture has much to say about how to deal with loss in a healthy way. Whether it is loss of a job, or a loved one, or a limb, we must go through the feeling of the loss. We must say good-bye to what we no longer have. For instance, revenge is the refusal to say good-bye to the hope of personal retribution. Likewise, holding on to our dead husband's clothes as though he is still alive, or talking about a past love affair as though we still have it, are typical of the lies we all live. There is no short cut to letting go. We must first face the truth, then allow the Holy Spirit to release the feelings, often of painful grief and loss. This will be followed by our need to say good-bye, as in naming the child from an abortion or miscarriage, giving them to the Lord. This will all happen in waves over a period of time. Finally, we must resolve to leave the circumstances with the Lord as we get on with our lives, making peace with the memories.*

During the next few months I learnt slowly but surely God's ways in many similar areas, welcoming much inner healing. 'Homework' had to become a daily routine. It was not a straightforward path, more like a roller-coaster ride. On more than one occasion I discovered that for several days I had been resisting something the Holy Spirit wanted to release. Either it was too sore, or I was too angry, or I had simply stopped giving time to listening. But the build-up of emotional pressure was so intense that I could not resist it for long. Once this cleansing has started we cannot stop it without standing against the Lord and becoming even more sick. There was always a sense of urgency and it was vital that I gave the necessary time to allow the cleansing to happen, even if the benefits felt so slow in coming.

Homework

Pursuing such healing in the midst of daily work and family commitments is really hard. But I knew nothing was more important than my ongoing healing. So I made it a strict practice to spend a minimum of one hour a day discovering the feelings and truth that would be so essential for my future. Sometimes this would be forcing the feelings out so tangibly that they would 'flood' me with their strength. I could spend all my homework crying, groaning or screaming into a pillow until I was exhausted. Other times I would discover a lie and my homework would be in repentance for having given it a place in my life. It was also a time for spiritual physiotherapy, looking at the mistakes I had made during the day and identifying an alternative response with the Holy Spirit's help for next time. Homework became a lifeline in my inner healing.

As I settled down again in England, knowing that my travelling was over for a while, the Lord made it clear that His healing in my life needed to remain my priority. It would be two-fold. The cleansing of my emotion and memories was to continue. But for the first time this would facilitate the release of healthy emotion and habit patterns in my life. I had much to learn. Throughout my life my emotion had been bound by a backlog of pain, anger, trauma, fear... It was not mine to enjoy. I had no conception of how to welcome and appreciate healthy emotion, because my feelings had never been free to grow with me. In fact, many of my emotions had got locked up in the time warp of my childhood. The Lord wanted to begin to teach me how He had designed them to operate. I felt like I was a three-year old girl in the body of a thirty year old woman – quite embarrassing really! I needed to start to learn to discipline my emotions to respond to the Holy Spirit under the Lordship of Christ, so they could become an integral part of the new person He was freeing me to become.

When I arrived back in Bromley I moved into a very old, dilapidated flat attached to an empty warehouse, soon to be demolished. It was a depressing environment, poorly heated, noisy, sparsely furnished with well-used hand-me-downs. But it was offered almost rent free by the mission that owned it and I had no money to afford anything else. It was here that the Lord wanted me to make myself at home – something I had never done before. I was alone and had to look after myself, to learn to take responsibility for myself. A significant part of the healing of the next few months came simply as I learnt the basic life skills that so many take for granted. None of these came naturally to me. But this was a place for me to express my new-found tastes, opinions and personality in my own home environment. I was to create a home for myself. And what better place to learn that home was an expression of who I was. I began to discover I did not need material possessions for it to be a home. If I was at home in myself then any place could become my home.

And on to another practicality. For the first time in two years I started worshipping regularly at church again. I went to a local charismatic fellowship that Peter and Mary belonged to. This too was difficult for me. The tension that had prevented me from being in church for so long was no longer there, but in its place I found an equally unbearable sensitivity to the presence of the Holy Spirit and the love of God. I found that opening myself to the Holy Spirit always brought on floods of tears, much to the embarrassment of the folk around me. It lasted several months. But I knew how critical it was for me to let the tears of healing flow, whenever they were triggered. I had no need to be ashamed of them. I must not switch them off and shut out the healing. I was not to get involved in church life – I was just to be there on Sundays. This was most unusual for me. But the Lord was jealous He remain my priority. There was to be no distraction from Him, not even a Christian one!

The other new beginning the Lord gave me was in my work. I had given no thought whatsoever to paid employment in my travels. I knew I needed work that would allow me to continue my healing, rather than drain my energies. Miraculously my financial resources had never run out in the fifteen months since leaving the NHS, even though I had no savings. But now the provision dried up. My ideal was to be self-employed by making use of my management skills and experience. I heard that a local Medical Mission were in need of a Management Consultant with my professional background. It became a very demanding job for the next year whilst I discovered so much of myself through my journey of inner healing.

After four months I heard that my little flat was going to be demolished and I would have to move out. Where to live next? With dismay, I heard the Lord confirm my worst fear – that He wanted me to move back home to live with Mum. I had not lived with Mum since my 'nervous breakdown' some eight years before, when Dad was still alive. The house was full of negative memories and associations. And my relationship with Mum had undergone such an extensive amount of change as the Lord had begun to heal me, that it was still strained. But no other door opened, so I yielded to the Lord.

A couple of days before I made the move, the Lord provided me with a gracious release, in an unusual and unexpected way. I had suffered a very disturbed sleep pattern for many years. It had never really settled after my 'breakdown' and had got noticeably worse with all the disturbances in my spirit during the healing. I had grown accustomed to waking five or six times a night, having taken perhaps an hour to get to sleep in the first place. But at the end of a church service the preacher said he had a word from the Lord about insomnia. For several minutes he described how sleep was something God wanted to give to His children and that Satan's intent was to disturb it. I agreed with him heartily. Then he asked everyone who wanted the Lord to free them from insomnia to stand. Along with perhaps twenty others in the hall I stood up. As he prayed, I found that I started to sob. I was aware that the Holy Spirit was touching me and bringing me cleansing from this burdensome oppression that I had carried for so long. Two days later when I moved back home, I slept right through the night for the first five nights I was there. What provision! The hold of the Enemy was broken. My sleep pattern could begin to heal. It was one of the few times in my journey of healing when the Holy Spirit healed me in a church service with a number of others.

Sleep

The Lord promises sleep to us all, but what I had not realised was that the sleep patterns I had made peace with were not what God intended. I began to learn that much happens to us as we sleep. Our spirit can be restored by the Lord along with our bodies. It also gives the Lord the opportunity to use dreams to talk to us, releasing knowledge about ourselves and others we did not consciously know. But sleep also symbolises rest in Christ – we are at peace with Him, we can trust His protection. I began to learn to take a notebook to bed, to empty my head of the day's affairs, giving it all to Him until morning, inviting Him to cleanse my spirit of all the debris of the day. Or I would anticipate a difficult task I faced the following day and commit this to Him, frequently finding I would wake in the morning with the solution. Sleep is a gift He wants to give all of us. He restores our soul.

7 Women And The Spiritual World

Inner healing felt so slow. And it was such hard work. It seemed interminable. Layer after layer of anger and pain was triggered during the day. Each evening I would let it out in my homework. I felt my healing was grinding to a halt. There were no major milestones, no significant times of ministry. And I had no way of measuring my progress. The only thing I could do was to cling blindly to the belief that if the feeling was still there, there was more healing still to come. So it was with shock one day that I realised that with every layer of pain and trauma, every old memory that upset me, every emotional battle I fought, the Holy Spirit was cleansing and lifting away the damage. The emotion of the different layers frequently felt the same, time and time again in fact, but it was really new healing each time, another wave of cleansing. I was frequently working with the same subject but different aspects of it. Far from going too slowly, my healing was happening so fast I was missing the significance of it!

Do We Ever Come To An End Of Healing?

I am often asked, 'How will I know when it has all gone?.' The answer is embarrassingly simple – when it is not there any more!! The key to this part of any person's healing is persistence, not being satisfied with second best. You will frequently have the feeling that you have been here before – that you have already dealt with this issue. The accuser will

> *suggest you did not deal with it properly last time, it failed. But hold your ground and keep on going. The issue may be self-hate and you will need to look at seven or eight aspects of this. Or it may be abuse or betrayal and you have several people you need to deal with. On occasions you may later understand the various layers. Other times you will never be told by the Lord, but the feelings will have gone anyway. Just be faithful. The journey is unique and different for every one of us. But patterns will emerge as to how the Lord walks the road with you. Much of this journey may be routine, but it will often lead to another issue that you have now earned the right to overcome.*

As well as my specific times of homework with the Lord, I had many battles with the well-established reflexes which had grown up around my baggage and now seemed to have a life of their own, despite the root of the damage having gone. Even though I knew I had been cleansed from the shamed and apologetic person I had become, when I met someone new I always 'instinctively' withdrew. When someone mistreated me in even the slightest way I seethed inside for days, instead of letting the anger go. Even in small and ridiculous ways the residue of the damage still tarnished my life – it was impossible to make a cup of coffee in the office without needing to make one for everyone else. My motive was not kindness but fear and a need for approval.

I realised that if I really wanted to become the woman that I had been created to be, I would need to dismantle these unrighteous behaviour patterns. Many of them were not wrong in themselves, but they were rooted in my unrighteous past, not in Christ and so they were sin. I began to choose one little detail of my life a week and specifically decide how I would like to change it. What was a righteous response? I would practice at home, unseen, until tentatively I would feel able to experiment in relationship. Taking the initiative to go and shake someone's hand instead of waiting for them to greet me. Or deferring to others when in a meeting, instead of taking control. In these small ways I began to grow into wholeness.

What Is Sin?

I was discovering that God's perspective on sin was very different to mine. I had thought that if I didn't 'do' anything that was wrong, then I wasn't living in sin. What a silly illusion! The truth was that much about me was the result of a life lived in denial, and this had become sin to me. For instance, the ways I 'protected' myself from other people hurting me, the shame I carried, my fear of life, my control of other people... all these were ways of my having power over my own and other people's lives. I was living in deceit, so much of what I did became sin to me. My lifestyle made it impossible for me to be honest and real, and this stood in the way of my becoming the person God had created me to be.

In my early childhood this way of life was the inevitable consequence of personal pain. God did not condemn me for this. But as I began my journey into healing I did not need to continue this lifestyle of denial and deceit. My baggage, lifestyle and reflexes all cut me off from my true self, who I was becoming in Christ, and this was sin. As I let go of more of my past, so I could lay down the sin which clung to it. God cannot have a relationship with my false selves.

Much of the focus for the changes in my life at this time was in my relationship with Mum. I was acutely aware that the reality of the healing I had received was being 'put to the test' with her. Would I be able to live as Susan, the woman I was becoming, or would I retreat to the Sue of my past, the girl I felt my mother still expected me to be? For the previous two years my mother had not commented on the changes in me and in my life. But now I was in her house, trying to live in new ways in an old environment. In spite of my progress in other areas I found myself getting more and more angry with her, increasingly frustrated at what I perceived to be the superficiality and hypocrisy in our relationship.

My home, the place in which I was living, no longer felt like a safe space in which I could freely pursue inner healing. I wanted to move out. I felt as if I would explode with the intensity of the ever-present conflict between my past and my future. But I had seen too much of God's arranging of circumstances in my healing. He clearly had a purpose in putting me in this hot house. He gave me no permission to leave.

One evening I poured my heart out to the Lord. How could I carry on? In my angry state I would end up obstructing God's purpose and would myself delay dealing with the next issue. The Lord had a very simple answer; 'Ask me for a measure of love for your mother.' That was a new idea. I had released the backlog of hurt and anger I had carried towards her for so many years. But I realised I did not love her. Within days I found myself in tears before the Lord, telling Him that I wanted to love her, for the simple reason that she was my mum. That was healing. In the weeks that followed I learnt to honour my mother in love. Our relationship was not close and indeed could not be, for we were two very different people. Love was not a substitute for truth and much of the truth remained painful, but in Christ, and only in Christ, love and truth can walk hand in hand.

Honouring Parents

All of us, if we are to walk the road of wholeness, will at one time or another have to confront the issue of parents. Very few of us seem to have good experiences, once the Lord begins to expose the damage in our lives. If we are not careful, we can easily get stuck here, under their spiritual authority and baggage. Ultimately we will need to separate ourselves from them spiritually, letting go of the past, and declare we are now part of the eternal family of God. This will not mean we need to personally confront them with all our dislikes. We should continue honouring them while moving away from our earthly inheritance and returning to our inheritance in Christ. In most instances this leads to an improvement in family relationships. We are free to love in the way that God intended us to.

As the weeks passed, various words, fears and pictures came, which were more ominous than the inner healing agenda I had been dealing with. This caused me yet another conflict. I was tempted to renounce the lies, the mocking of the darkness, the smell of death. I had seen Christ take authority over Satan's claim for my life and I thought that chapter of my healing was ended. Yet I had learnt not to use 'faith' to suppress things coming to the surface in my spirit, but rather to let my spirit speak freely to me. When I did so, I could feel a recurring fear of men. I knew it affected my relationship with God, since I (wrongly) perceived God as male. In spite of the new love I had found for my mother I also carried an instinctive fear of her which I just couldn't undo. I discovered this fear filled relationships with certain types of women and with many men. I had become accustomed to areas of pain and damage being completely healed after homework, but I had an instinctive despising and contempt of people which didn't go, even when I repented. I also experienced a lot of physical pain. Some was part of the cleansing of my spirit, but some also confirmed the growing awareness I had that there was a further obstruction the Lord would need to deal with in due course.

I was also very frustrated that whilst learning much about myself, I seemed to have come to a standstill in my relationship with the Lord. I was discovering me, not God. I was tempted to blame myself. The 'accuser of the brethren' was not missing the opportunity. I felt under a cloud, cut off from the Lord and was totally unable to rest in my relationship with Him. I continued to go to church and cried most of the time whilst there. They were still tears of healing, even though tinged with self-pity and confusion as I was faced with the barrenness of my life and my relationship with the Lord.

The only issue that I could see was to do with fathering. Shortly after grieving for my father, I was dismayed to discover that I was grieving again – this time totally irrationally for the baby that had been burnt on the beach in my bloodline. This felt very odd, as if it was 'my baby'... Surely not? I was attending a conference in London on Holiness and was overwhelmed. For the first time in twelve months, I found a team of people praying for me. They knew nothing about me – I think they thought I had had an abortion. It was so real. I set my offended mind to one side and just followed my feelings. Within a week, the grief had all gone.

But I was left with the feeling that Satan had fathered my child. Also, that Satan had 'fathered' me. I was astounded to realise my 'common sense' told me that Satan was my father. Therefore God could never be my Father because I already had one! Even worse was the reality that there was a part of me that didn't want to let go of this perverse fathering. This was gross. I had to acknowledge the truth of how I felt and say sorry to Father God that I didn't want Him.

The Companionship Of Baggage

With long term damage we all make a friend of our baggage. We have to, or the conflict would drive us mad. We adjust our lifestyle to accommodate our baggage. Sometimes we will dissociate this part of us, other times consciously allow it to become part of our life. This makes it virtually impossible for the Lord to take the damage, because part of us believes it belongs to us, so we hold onto it tightly! This is such a hard lesson for many of us. We must gradually see the lie that it is part of us and begin instead to practice repentance for the 'appendage' we have created. We must separate ourselves and stand against it with Christ. The biggest battle for most of us will be seeing the sin for what it is – an intruder. We will then need to declare that we are genuinely willing to live without it. This will be another big battle. Can we face the temporary barrenness of living without the baggage?

Several days later my 'sorry' had grown enough for me to do some spiritual surgery, affirming the Fatherhood of God and giving my love and worship only to Him. I had to separate myself from the patterns of manipulation and control given to me by my former 'father', laying down the evil 'power' which I felt I had in the spiritual realms. Afterwards there was a terrible feeling of loss. I grieved. I could feel more of the old 'Sue' and its energy fading away. Once again I found myself wondering who I would be without these powers and voices. I declared to the Lord that I wanted to find out. I invited more of the Lordship of Christ over my mind.

It had been a year since the claims on my life had been so vividly exposed. Why were they surfacing again? I was grateful to the Lord that by this stage in the healing journey I knew more than to question whether this was just a repeat of the previous year. If the Lord was turning His attention to those pictures again, it was because He had a new work to do in relation to them. I realised that in the past I had been very badly confused over the issue of Lordship. I was aware of all the demands of the Enemy as lord in my life, his manipulation and control, the guilt, the abuse of me for his own purposes. I had assumed that any lord required slavery and was devastated to discover that I had imputed to Christ the same extortionate demands. I had to ponder the truth that with Jesus as my Lord, He wanted only the best for me. His Lordship of my life was not for His own ends, but in order to release my life to me. If I then chose to give that life back to Him, He would receive it gladly. But if not, there was no coercion, no manipulation, no conditions. I had to repent of treating my Lord Jesus as if He 'lorded it over me' like Satan had. I asked Him to show me what true Lordship meant in the Kingdom of God.

Lordship

The crucifixion of Christ and His victory over death and Satan allows us to choose and change masters. If we have Satan as our master it is for bondage and slavery. But if we have Christ as Master I began to see it is for freedom and choice. Just like in the Gospels, Christ heals us in order to let us go, so we can then come back to Him if we wish, to worship, love and adore Him freely. At the beginning of my journey into healing I clearly had two Lords, both making very different demands on me. It was not enough to slip from one to the other. I had to let the perversion of lordship die completely and then begin learning what true Lordship was.

Welcoming Christ as Lord stirred up my desire to be baptised. But as I prepared for it, I faced an excessive amount of fear and began having all kinds of strange dreams. I even considered postponing it to another time, but I could not think of a good enough reason for doing so. I began to appreciate the poignant significance of the symbolism of baptism. In going under the water I would be taking with me all the death that belonged to the old 'Sue'. But in rising from the water I would be leaving it behind. It was a statement of faith that I wanted to be buried with Christ, be washed by the waters and rise again a new creation. The claim of evil on my life was against my old person, Sue. As I died in Christ, the authority of the claim would also die, because the person it applied to in the spiritual world was dead. I knew I was not yet completely free for it to fully happen, but I was standing in faith in the place I knew the Lord was taking me to. I would do my part.

The service was great – the first time I had shared my testimony in the UK. It was a good reminder of all that God had done in rescuing me. I had been a Christian for fifteen years and felt as if maybe I was just about to start knowing myself and God. As I came up out of the water I felt a familiar evil shudder – the spiritual reality of the act of baptism had not gone unnoticed. I had carried a conflict of allegiance for so long, tearing me apart in my spirit. But now I could give myself to my Lord Jesus more fully than ever before – or could I?

Although the inner healing continued after my baptism, the nightmares I had begun to have grew even more clear, obviously related to bloodline issues again. I ground to a halt in my homework and lost my focus. It felt like there was a huge evil anger that was being directed at me.

Peter and Mary were abroad for a month, my management consultancy work was about to end, my relationship with the Lord was nowhere to be found and I felt very dirty. I even started getting physically sick, strange pains, tiredness... I tumbled into a depression the like of which I hadn't known for several years. I felt full of hate, anger, rebellion, bitterness. My mind was in chaos. I went through three months of terrible doubt – was God really going to heal me? Perhaps none of it had worked after all and I had just been deceiving myself and all those around me.

Deepest Darkness Just Before The Dawn

Like the last lap of a marathon, it is very common for folk to go through a time where they get significantly worse immediately before dealing with a major issue. This had been true in my case several times. The darkness overwhelms us, the death consumes us and we give up. This is where the Lord needs us to give all things to Him and persevere. Even though I knew it, I never really adjusted to the uncomfortable reality that it will get worse before it gets better. It feels as though God is betraying us, or we are betraying ourselves. Yet to engage the real sickness we are about to let go it must first be exposed. Many Christians do not understand this pattern and even fight it, but this was often the Lord's way with me. I always came through it.

At one point the Enemy whispered such a terrible and gross lie to me, that it startled me out of the despondency. It felt as if the 'strong man' was the only one who had ever looked after me, caressed me, taught me to live and loved me! When this one surfaced it was like a brief blast of fresh air. I rebuked the lie in Jesus' Name and declared that I was loved by God. I did not know what His purposes were, but I could know that they were full of love. If the Lord was not bringing me healing, He had a good reason. In this and other occasional shafts of light during this time, I realised that if I was struggling so hard, the end of the Lord's work must be in sight. This excessive depression was a thorough distraction of the Enemy and was the Holy Spirit exposing Satan's remaining influences. But most of the time I had no such confidence. Life was very miserable.

I did discuss how I was feeling with Peter and Mary but they said if there was anything left to deal with, now was not the time. They were quite right to wait and the delay undoubtedly allowed the Lord to put everything in place for an almighty victory. I did not need to see the preparations – if I had it would not have been any easier to wait. I just had to endure.

Very suddenly, on Easter Monday five months after my baptism, the timing appeared right. At less than twenty-four hours notice, Peter and Mary invited two others to join us. I wrote up a set of background notes of what I felt the issues were. In the chaos and confusion I had not seen too clearly, but I had found a new element to the pictures from my bloodline which had never been significant before – the presence of a woman. It was the woman who had given up her daughter to the 'man' and then sacrificed her offspring on the beach. The woman was a 'high priestess', who had given her daughter over to a living death, condemned to live, not free to die. She had also given up her grandson in death. Suddenly I saw that she was the one with the authority in all the rituals in the woods. Every time the 'man' would leave or be banished from the scene, she would invite him back again. Even more than the 'man' involved in the rape, I found a terrifying fear of the woman who was orchestrating the proceedings.

Repenting On Behalf Of Others

In areas of bloodline sin I found it essential to be willing to repent of the sin of my forebears as if it were my own. I had not done any of it. It had not been done to me. But the effective release of the healing to me was dependant on it being covered by the blood of Christ. Someone, sometime would need to repent. As God reveals the sin from His perspective its weight is crushing and the repentance is heartfelt. It was the ministry of the Old Testament prophets and even of Christ, to repent of sin other than their own. To repent we do not need to be guilty ourselves, but just to feel the sin as God does.

Unlike previous sessions it was not sufficient for the team praying with me to affirm my decision and renounce the Enemy's lies and claims. This time I had to renounce the family claim. First I had to repent of all the sin of my bloodline, as if it was my own. Bringing such evil to the Cross produced great turmoil. Only then could I take up the sword of the Spirit so that I could sever the ropes that bound me to the Enemy. Many times even this was difficult and required an intense exertion of my spirit. But as I cut the ropes I renounced the claims in Jesus' Name and had to turn away to the Cross and choose the light. So the way became clear for the Lord to move through my bloodline and expose the evil intent over my life.

The key in the session was when the woman was commanded to reveal herself from her hiding place. She was very evil and had given Satan the sacrifice of the baby. I had tremendous fear of her authority and her intent. The men paled into insignificance as her towering presence was exposed. I cried out to the Lord for the courage to turn away from her and find my protection in His Lordship. And gradually it came. She did not weaken, but the all-powerful presence of Christ in His Holiness broke through to rescue me from the clutches of death as I chose His Life.

After the woman's authority in my life had been broken by the Lord, and after a few minutes rest, the Holy Spirit began to release another series of pictures to cleanse my spirit. They were all related to womanhood – issues of life and death. The Holy Spirit was being very thorough in releasing the cleansing of the blood of Christ to every area, allowing none of it to remain hidden. Several times it was so gross that I did not want to continue, but the team encouraged me and the Lord required it of me. Throughout the ministry one of the team read Scriptures specifically declaring how the Lord wanted to redeem His holy purposes and expose all that the Enemy had sought to possess. I reached out for the promises in my spirit.

This session was the unveiling of an unrighteous female power over my life. Without undoing the authority it carried against God and myself, it would have permission to continue wreaking havoc in my spirit. And the benefit of the healing I had experienced to that time would have been gradually eroded and stolen. But although I was totally unaware of those authorities, the Lord knew. Whilst I had been considering abandoning my healing, so severe was the confusion, He was patiently and deliberately preparing me for the hardest session that would finally expose the worst of my baggage.

I began to understand more clearly why I had been living with Mum in the preceding months and why the Holy Spirit had focused so much on my family and on issues of fathering in His preparatory inner healing. If there had been festering bitterness and resentment in these relationships and memories, I would have been hindered in my spirit in repenting on behalf of all my family throughout the generations. And the session would have been far harder, if not totally wasted. Our daily faithful obedience gives the Lord the opportunity to give us far more.

I saw specific patterns in the lives of my family that I now needed to refute. There was no honouring of womanhood in my bloodline. There was a pattern of manipulative and jealous relationships with an ungodly matriarchal authority. My mother's parents had an unhappy marriage, ending in divorce in the 1960s. My father's mother died when he was young, abandoning him to an alcoholic father. Although my parents hid the damage well, their own difficulties only exacerbated the damage that was being passed on through the generations in both bloodlines.

I began to look with new understanding at male-female relationships and was horrified to see how women control men. Sometimes it was overt – a strong woman dominating a damaged man. But more shocking was the hidden reality in the spiritual world of women secretly hating and despising men whilst outwardly appearing to care for them. I had genuinely thought I loved men but deep in my spirit I had been attacking these 'pathetic little creatures', as I perceived them to be. The belief in female superiority was innate and unquestioned. The revenge I carried against men for all they did to women was not my revenge, but something I had picked up in my spirit from my bloodline. These expectations were then reinforced by abuse during my childhood and just buried more deeply beneath a veneer of brotherly love when I became a Christian.

God-Man-Woman

This ministry session and the build-up to it was in many ways the most disturbing of all, as it turned upside-down all that I presumed about male-female relationships. Even in the church I had been taught women were the vulnerable ones being exploited by strong and sometimes evil men. But from the spiritual dimension woman took on a very different role. Scripture and society show her as the one with the spiritual attunement, more than men, having entered into a direct relationship with Satan (Genesis 3). She is now more actively involved in spiritual things.

When God created man in His own image as man and woman, then took woman out of man, it was for life-giving companionship, both physically and spiritually. But I had been attacking men from my spirit – hurting and despising them without either them or I consciously knowing what was happening. Men around me were the victims of this spiritual betrayal. I was incapable of giving them life from my spirit. The women of my past were the real masters, inspired by the Enemy of both man and woman and I had also taken up the tools of their warfare, thinking this was womanhood. As my ministry has developed, working especially with broken marriages, I have been able to help many women discover how they hate, revenge and manipulate men spiritually. It is a hidden spiritual dimension of male-female relationships. Men are not always to blame in the failure of marriage. Women carry a spiritual armoury which, though unseen, can be lethal in any relationship they are involved in, giving death instead of life to all those around them.

I had often wondered whether I would clearly recognise when the final demonic stronghold in my life was broken. The answer was yes. At the end of the session and in the following days, there was no doubt that the vile claims of the Enemy had been covered with the blood of Christ and rendered ineffective. When I broke my allegiance with the women of my bloodline, I felt a 'fresh air' in my spirit, even in the midst of the exhaustion from the session. And I was aware of a dignity birthed in the excitement of knowing that my many personal and private struggles throughout thirty years of life had a rational source from which I was free at last. I now know in significant detail what the Enemy's plan for my life was. But it is a purpose that Christ has rescued me from – I owed Him my life.

8 Traumatic Memories

Overnight the terrible oppression and dark depression to which I had succumbed was gone. I was healed. What did it feel like to be healed? Terrible! I had expected to have a wonderful feeling of 'wholeness' and to be dynamically in love with the Lord at the end of such an intensive journey of healing. Surely with the final roots of the oppression gone, I would become mature in the Lord, able to radically enjoy my new-found freedom and ready to live life. I wanted to gallop into the fullness of my healing. But instead I was in the midst of intense after-shock. And the feeling was far more devastating than after any other session. I began to feel that with all the baggage in my life banished, there was nothing of me left. In our ministry we call it the 'empty box syndrome'.

Being Healed But Empty

In our ministry today we are able to minimise the impact of this post-surgery shock by teaching a more gradual daily way of pursuing our wholeness. But for many of us there will be times of significant authority shifts in our spirit, following ministry, that we are left feeling very disorientated for a time. In the past our baggage will have given us an unrighteous energy which we presumed upon. There is, therefore, no substitute for time, following intense surgery, to allow our bodies to adjust to life without the unrighteous drives, and for the Holy Spirit to birth new ways of wholeness in us. We must make peace with the emptiness for a season.

This emptiness lasted several months. Of course I should have expected it. No-one goes through life-giving surgical intervention without taking months to recover while learning to possess their healing. The sense of anti-climax was unbearable. Three years of all-consuming healing had been completed, only to leave me feeling more cut off from the Lord and from myself than I had been before I started. Realising that for the first time in my life all the evil had been wiped off the board and my life was a clean sheet did not seem to help. I could only see that the sheet was very empty and that was intimidating. For some time I could not comfortably be in the Lord's presence, because of the painful reminders it brought of the surgery I had so recently undergone. When I thought of blood, I saw the blood of the baby. When I thought of Lord, I remembered the lordship of my old master. I had to let it all go for a while. I stopped my times of homework. I allowed myself to become absorbed in the daily routine of life. I sensed that this pleased the Lord. My spirit had undergone a terrible shock, was very fragile and needed to remain untouched and unexposed for a while.

Yet again my life on a practical level was mirroring the state of my spirit. I was staggered by the fact that within a week of this last session I had a chance to move out from living with Mum and 'house-sit' a four-bedroomed house. I had no furniture, no kitchen equipment, no bedding – my house was as barren as my life felt. I borrowed the basics such as a bed and a small fridge and cooked with a microwave and an electric frying pan. I was given an armchair and when entertaining, got out a garden chair! And I supplemented all this with the luxury of a rented television and video. Of course, my new-found furniture did not go very far in such a large house, but it was sufficient. The Lord was providing for my needs. I enjoyed having my own space and began to practice being at home in it.

My house was not to be empty for very long. At the beginning of my healing the Lord had promised that He would meet all my needs and not allow me to lose out by forsaking my job in obedience to Him. Four months after I had moved in, in yet another fulfilment of that promise, the empty shell which had been my home was amply furnished, even colour co-ordinated, as I was given a 'housefull' of furniture from a show-flat. The Lord was continuing to prove Himself abundantly faithful.

Combined with the rigours of setting up home, my daily life was also filled with the demands of beginning work again – two consultancies simultaneously for related missions. That was really hard. Meeting new people, carrying responsibility when I felt as if I couldn't even meet with the Lord was a huge risk. But the Lord was pushing me on. No hiding, no holding back. Slowly I began to undertake just a little inner healing – there were new areas for the Holy Spirit to heal and redeem which He had chosen not to touch until that final bloodline authority from the woman had been banished. More spiritual house-cleaning. I saw a picture of an angel with a broom, cleaning out one room after another, from time to time passing the broom to me when I had to actively get rid of the dirt myself.

Just over three months after that amazing session in which the Lord broke through the strongholds of the bloodline, I found myself preparing for a five week business trip. My consultancy work was taking me to the Central Asian Republics of the Soviet Union, as it was then, and Pakistan. I was terrified. God wasn't just pushing back boundaries here – this was taking me way beyond any known comfort zone!

The trip was very demanding. I had become used to travelling during my pursuit of healing, but had not been to Asia, or to countries where no-one had any English. I could not speak any Russian or Uzbek, so communication was interestingly creative! In Pakistan, the cultural barriers to women were more of a problem than the language barrier. I was grateful that the Lord had brought some cleansing to my womanhood before I left. He was using the trip as a training ground for me professionally, whilst also continuing the on-going work of cleansing and inner healing in my personal life. Many times I struggled with intense fear and was heavily dependant on the Lord for my every provision. But it was a real education, very humbling and after five weeks of a very steep learning curve I came back delighted that the Lord and I had coped so well!

One of the most significant things to happen after I returned from my business trip was that I had permission from the Lord to begin to get more involved in ordinary church life. I had been tentatively and occasionally attending a weekly housegroup for some months but now found myself becoming part of a small church planting team. In a group of twenty, working closely together in evangelism and prayer, I began to find the courage to participate more fully in relationships and to find a way of contributing spiritually to the group. It was hard to do, for no-one knew of the unusual way in which the Lord had worked in my life. I found it very difficult to participate without wanting to attend every meeting and meet every need. For the first time in four years I joined a worship group again, very nervously and gradually, determined by God's grace to do so in new ways, not old. The opportunity of being part of such a small team was a gift from the Lord. But even here things did not stand still for long.

Several months after my summer in Central Asia I travelled to Cyprus to stay with a friend. It was the first

Christmas I had ever been away from home and that in itself brought healing. I had a chance to choose for myself how I wanted to celebrate new traditions among new people. And as my management consultancy contracts had just ended it was the ideal place to consider my future before the Lord. I spent many hours sitting in the sun on the flat roof of the apartment, or walking down to the beach and along the promenade, asking the Lord what to do with my life. What was important? The opportunities excited me. I knew that regardless of what I wanted, I would need to provide for myself so that I could buy a home. Even if I subsequently travelled to the mission field, my home could then be a base to which I could return. But the Lord was not telling me the priorities. They were mine to choose although He would help in the process of self-discovery. I needed to recognise who I was and own my responsibilities and choices for the first time in my life. In His relationship with us the Lord does not wish to dictate terms or restrict our path.

Guidance

I had taken a holiday to seek God's 'guidance'. With some shock I heard Him say that He really didn't mind what I did. In fact, it was as if He had specifically given me choices. What did I want to do? Here was another major lesson coming! How often we get into terrible bondage over an issue of guidance, trying to decide what God wants, waiting for Him to make His will clear. But in many cases God's will is not a tightrope but a chess-board. He merely wants to sit back and wait for us to tell Him what we want. He has already given us the great commission, as well as intellects, opinions, gifting, life. He wants us to act like adults in our relationship with Him; to just get on with it and honour Him as we do. It is not so much what we do as why we do it that is of relevance to the Lord, for He will use any situation and any decision we make, if we let Him, to increase our maturity. If He does want to comment on the decision He will, providing our spirit is open to His voice. I began to see that frequently our demand for guidance is simply an abdication of our God-given responsibility for ourselves. The Lord wanted me to grow up. In fact, my healing depended on it. If I was not prepared to be responsible for myself, how could I be responsible for what He was yet to give me?

I decided to extend my management experience and help Peter launch new businesses. I would make my work my priority after my relationship with the Lord and any further healing He wanted to release. Surely there could be nothing else to be healed? Yet whilst considering my future I was noticing a puzzling fear which was beginning to press in on me. I had found a new hunger for the Lord in Cyprus – for Him to be glorified through me, that I might grow into the woman He had created me to be. But in spite of this there was no rest in my spirit and the fear began troubling me.

Within days of returning from my holiday I realised that the fear resembled the agoraphobia I had suffered subsequent to my 'breakdown'. I began to feel a new wave of sadness and depression from my mother's bloodline. I saw how manipulation had been exercised under the guise of weakness and that tears had been a fundamental part of that strategy to incite sympathy. What a way to begin a new year. Within a few days some of the events that had occurred at the time of my 'breakdown' started coming vividly to mind and disturbing me. The Holy Spirit was exposing yet another area the Lord wanted to deal with.

It was obvious, though it had not occurred to me, that the confusion, pain and destructive behaviour patterns that had surrounded my 'breakdown' had never been the subject of the Holy Spirit's attention. Over the next two weeks the Lord took me back to the most traumatic months of my life. He had released me from evil authority which had been the hidden cause of the utter devastation of my breakdown. Now He wanted to heal the damage I was still carrying from two years of sickness and five years of drug dependency. I was terrified of touching the trauma of my breakdown – the fear in itself was clear evidence healing was still needed. I had hidden in bed in a suicidal despair, sleeping for three months, crippled with agoraphobia for two years. During that time I had concluded that for some reason God was not able to love, heal or protect me, though I never blamed God, only myself. How could I face letting all of these feelings and agonising memories come to the surface again? But, of course, if I didn't let the feelings go the Lord could not heal them.

I talked the matter through thoroughly with Peter and Mary, who confirmed what I was feeling from the Lord. He now wanted to bring healing to these memories. They agreed to help me. Naively I hoped that the Lord would only need to heal one or two root issues, rather than touch the volume of pain which I'd experienced. I was wrong. The Lord in His sovereign and gracious wisdom wanted to cleanse me from it all, so that it could not be used by the Enemy to weaken me in the future.

Dealing with this issue was somewhat different from any other phase of my healing, because it was an actual personal memory. Most of the other root issues the Lord had touched and healed had been laid on me by others or were a direct result of evil curses. The defensive mechanisms which had allowed me to declare during the worst moments of my deliverance that this baggage was not mine, no longer applied. My breakdown had happened to me.

Unexpectedly the Holy Spirit began by asking me to forgive those who had deeply hurt me and who were associated with the confusion that had triggered my breakdown. I was surprised that even after two years of practising laying down revenge I still struggled to forgive them. They had been one of the channels of so much destruction in my life. To even think of them still filled me with trauma. The lie of the Enemy that if I forgave them I was condoning their actions was again being whispered in my ear. I had to re-learn that in forgiving them I was not excusing them, but I was cutting myself free from them so that God could both heal me and deal justly with them. As I reminded myself of the truth, my heart responded and the lie was gone. I forgave them and gave the judgement of their actions to God.

At Peter's suggestion I wrote out a list of words and phrases which I had spoken frequently during my breakdown that had now become self-curses. It was the first time I saw in my own life the spiritual strength that is released against us when our own words and thoughts invite havoc into our lives. Even though I had long since stopped saying these things, their authority remained, until I repented of them. There were twelve phrases which were the most poignant, affecting my attitude to life (I didn't want it), my mind (I'm mad), and the escape mechanisms I used (I don't want anyone near me, I want to sleep). Even to identify the curses was deeply painful, because it took me back to the chaos and irrationality of the life I was trapped in at that time. In exposing the words and choices I had made I also felt the weight of depression that had caused them. I added to the list those words which had been spoken to me at the time that had a destructive authority which reinforced my own bad attitudes. And I felt some of the issues I had struggled with; being out of touch with reality, out of control of my mind, confusion as to what was truth and what was deceit...

Self Curses

At some time in their healing almost everyone will need to deal with this issue. We suggest they write out a list, inviting the Holy Spirit to quicken their memory. Most begin by denying they have any, but God is very eager to help us with this! Typically a person will come up with twenty to forty self-curses. It is not usually enough to just renounce or 'cut yourself off' from them. Many of these curses will be strong and toxic, requiring a deep personal repentance that is felt, not thought. We must see and feel the sin of what we and others have done. And we are not just breaking their power and intent, but their future consequences. Replacing the curse with righteous truth often takes weeks of practice. This will rarely be possible until we have dealt spiritually with the reason we welcomed the curse in the first place.

As well as the words and curses I also had to renounce the behaviour patterns that I adopted when I used sleep as a retreat from pain. This had opened my mind to be overcome with destructive thoughts of suicide. It felt like a black living mass of lies. I was appalled to discover that this was the way I thought my mind really was! But yet again the Holy Spirit reached into the dark places of my mind, bringing the light of Christ. He began to replace the confusion with truth, despair with hope, chronic depression with joy. I declared that I wanted to reclaim myself from the wreckage of my breakdown. I reaffirmed my choice to accept and learn to love myself. It was one of the few sessions where I could feel freedom coming during the prayer, rather than simply feeling the pain going.

The next day I woke with a startling improvement in my mind – I had not been able to think clearly in months. But the Holy Spirit was not finished. He was turning His attention to my emotion. During my breakdown, negative feelings had been so intense that I had cut myself off from them. Now the Lord required that I welcome my emotion back, releasing the backlog and cleansing them. My initial list was of seventeen negative and damaging feelings that had overcome me at various times. I had cursed my emotion. It took me all day to identify them, own them and declare I did not want this toxic pain.

It was such a traumatic time. For a forty-eight hour period I relived my breakdown in detail and experienced the depth of the fears and despair. The Lord required I enter into this fully, because He wanted to heal me fully from it. I was obedient to His insistence and He was faithful to my cries.

My self-acceptance grew quite instinctively after this release. As it did I became more and more hungry for the release of the spiritual gifting which I knew the Lord had given me. Until then I had not sought God for it. Quite the opposite – I did not really want the responsibility that it would bring! But this feeling was changing and I began talking to the Lord about it as the Holy Spirit stirred my spirit. However, with this I began to notice occasional words and dreams of a sexual nature. It did not occur to me that these were in some way associated with my spiritual gifting, but yet the more I talked with the Lord about my gifting and welcomed it, the louder the perverse sexual pictures became. I am amazed that after going through so much healing I did not see the connection. It never occurred to me that by gently prompting me to explore my gifts, the Lord was beginning to uncover the last remaining obstacle standing in the way of my complete healing.

Welcoming my gifting was in part about reclaiming it from the Enemy, to whom it had been given in my bloodline. Two years earlier in my healing, the presence of evil had been exposed to me through the use of colours. Now the Lord was redeeming this and releasing my gifting to me through colours. That morning we saw several treasure chests, each of which had an evil angel sitting on top. The evil presence left just as soon as it was told to go. It had no authority to remain. As the first chest was opened by the Lord I saw a colour which introduced me to one part of who the Lord wanted me to become. This was followed by a second colour, which the Lord touched with a shaft of light in my spirit. I felt its transformation. And so it continued. But as the repossession of spiritual gifting continued, so the unrighteous pictures also began to feel more real.

In a certain amount of confusion I talked with Peter about both the gifting and the sexual perversions which had been exposed. I acknowledged my fear of men, their sexuality and also of my own. And as I did so the fear increased to a startling intensity. I affirmed that I did not want the fear. We decided that the Lord had not finished releasing the gifting that He wanted and we should give Him a further opportunity. With a friend that evening we began to pray further.

I had absolutely no clue of what the Lord was about to do. I had no knowledge and no advance warning that the Holy Spirit was about to lead me through one of the most intensely difficult areas of my healing. That evening initiated ten hours of ministry over a forty-eight hour period, the Lord 'bringing back to my memory' the fact that I had been raped when I was around six years old. This was one of the reasons that the Lord had required me relive my 'breakdown'. It had been to help me practise engaging memories and touching their pain. If I had not already learnt submission in the releasing of memories, I would probably have never found the courage to allow the memory of the rape back into my life.

Sexual Abuse

Child sexual abuse is one of society's worst crimes. It is a breach of trust that not only assaults the body of a child but also the human spirit. But over the years I have learnt not to place too much importance on the memories, but to follow the pathway of the underlying emotion. This is because many of our memories are reconstructed so are no longer factually accurate, even with the Holy Spirit's help in healing. And some of the most traumatic abuse occurs in the human spirit without any physical act. Healing from such abuse will require a physical engaging of the emotion, which speaks more truth than the memory, but this must also be accompanied by the laying down of revenge. As part of our ministry we have been able to help many to let go of such damage 'just as if it never happened'.

It seems incredible to me now that I had no conscious knowledge, not even a hint, that the rape had occurred. There had been many times during the healing journey when I had asked the question. The amount and nature of the damage in my life all pointed to the fact that I had been the victim of sexual abuse. But I appeared to have no conscious recollection of it ever happening. As the revelation of the evil practices in my bloodline had become clear, I had assumed that all the sexual perversion I 'saw' had come from those earlier generations.

So that evening when we began praying, I began to open my spirit, expecting to receive more of the gifting the Lord wanted to release. But as I was asking the Lord for the next colour, I had great difficulty seeing it. Instead I began seeing pictures of the rape again, but these were different. No longer was it in the woods in darkness, but a street in daylight and more startling, it was a street that I recognised. For a long time I paused. The team sat quietly, waiting for me to speak out the picture that I could see. Peter could see it too, but said he would not speak it out for me. I had to own it for myself. My response was that it couldn't be true, my mind was playing tricks on me – this was getting ridiculous. If it was ridiculous, why not speak it out anyway, they said, so that they could agree with me! But I didn't want to. There was a sickening fear sweeping through my mind and body. This time I did not want to go any further. I waited for the picture to go away, but it didn't. It only grew in reality. I began to go into shock, still not having spoken a word of what I was seeing. I knew the Lord was not going to allow me to avoid this, whatever it was. I continued to declare vehemently that it was all wrong and not real. It was just my warped imagination. But I began to answer their questions as they spoke them.

The first questions were innocuous enough. What was the weather like? Where was the event happening? Who was in it? What was I wearing? I could see myself so vividly as a little girl, skipping down a side-street, going to play with a friend. So who else could I see? A young man, standing in the street in front of me, outside his house. I knew who he was. All the children in the neighbourhood lived in fear of him, always running away when he came into the street. But he was standing in my way, looking at me.

I began to relive what happened next. The Holy Spirit had unlocked memories I had buried within days of the event, but which were now surfacing very quickly. The only hindrance was my willingness. I was struggling to find the courage to acknowledge what I was seeing. As I spoke out one detail they encouraged me to seek the next. The memory built gradually but was crystal clear.

During that evening I saw part of the picture. But it took four hours for me to be able to declare that I could 'remember' standing in front of this man, too frightened to run away. He had exposed himself to me as I tried to pass him in the street and he took hold of me. I was frozen in fear and unable to cry out or struggle. He had started feeling me, kissing me. I remembered him touching me, looking at me. I could hear him talking to me, threatening me not to move, telling me I would enjoy it, laughing at me, mocking me. But more than just the memory I could actually feel it happening. That's how I knew it was real. It was terrible. After four hours reliving the memory, I still did not know that he had raped me. I knew that I had been sexually abused and I felt disgusted. But the Lord gave me permission to stop, to 'surface' from the memories for a while. In huge shock and trauma I did so, but we acknowledged that there was more prayer needed to finish the ministry.

The next day I went to work as usual. But I felt dirty and ashamed. I needed a day to get through the initial shock before I was able to remember the horrific details of what happened next. The following evening a different friend joined us, to help seek the final release of the incident. Again it took four hours, again I resisted much of the way, unwilling to acknowledge the truth. When we began, I adamantly denied that anything further had happened. But the Lord was not prepared to 'save' me from the truth of the incident. He did not want to condemn me to live with the suppressed trauma for the rest of my life. It was suggested that if nothing further had happened we would quit. But we would go through it again, just to be sure. This time there was a gap. I could not piece together the details between two parts of the incident. I tried to remember, but it did not come easily. Gradually I felt more of what had happened. Even as I described it I would not accept that I had actually been raped. I just spoke out the feelings, then I remembered. Immediately after the first rape, there had been a second, then a third. Each was a little different, I could 'see' it very clearly. Only when I had relived the whole incident and we knew there were no more gaps, did those praying with me allow me to stop. It was incredibly painful, but it was over. It *had* taken place and I *had* now recalled it all.

I had been the victim of a violent prolonged rape, on a summer's afternoon in a street near my home. I was six or seven years old. In my childish naiveté, I had no understanding at all at the time of what had happened. I did not even know what rape was. I knew afterwards that I felt in terrible physical pain and very dirty. But throughout the whole incident I had been terrified to look at what was happening, so had stared straight ahead. I knew what it felt like, but I did not know what it was. I went home and remember Mum asking me a question or two, but nothing more. How could I tell anyone? What would I say? So in accordance with the practice that was by then already firmly established in my life, I said nothing. The event held such trauma that my mind quickly suppressed the feelings and memories. That which I had felt so vividly would have been locked away for ever, if the Lord had not intervened. But graciously He required I relive the incident in all the detail I had suppressed at the time. Only in this way could all the trauma be cleansed from my life. And it was the Holy Spirit who had helped quicken the memory, bringing it to the surface.

In the days that followed I felt terrible. It was just as if the rape had happened the previous day. The multitude of feelings I was unable to release at the time began to surface. Peter insisted that I came to work for at least part of the next day, although my choice would have been to stay inside my house and not see anyone. I felt extreme shame. I could feel the rape and its associated filth in my body – it was as if everyone could see it. I walked with shame and fear along the pavement, clinging to the wall. It was only after a few days the 'memory' of the feelings began to ease. But it was to be many weeks before I could go out and be around men without feeling intensely vulnerable. As with my breakdown, this was an incident that had actually happened to me. The Holy Spirit could not remove its effects merely by releasing me from the bloodline in which it was rooted. The damage of the incident was deeply ingrained and would take time to heal.

The further perversion of the incident was that at the end of the rape I glimpsed a moving curtain in the house in which the man lived. His mother had seen it all. It was as if she had given me to him. This was totally in accordance with my bloodline, where the damage appeared to have been done by the 'strong man' but was in fact 'authorised' by a woman. I found letting go of my revenge and fear of her even more difficult than that of the man who had raped me.

Of course, if I had been organising my own healing, I think I would have dealt with the huge issue of rape first! But in fact the Lord had already healed many of the consequences of it during the previous years of ministry. My self-image, my womanhood, my sense of shame, my attitude to relationships – these were all areas of personal damage. The Holy Spirit had brought a significant cleansing to them. He only required that I face the truth of the incident and let go of the remaining trauma, pain and emotional damage. Then the healing could be released in these areas too.

This incident explained many fears, attitudes and responses as I was growing up. My trauma over body hair suddenly made sense. My fear of my own sexuality, the feeling that sex was dirty, my shame over nakedness. Several times during my teens and twenties I had been in situations where men had exposed themselves to me. I now saw I was unwittingly sexually attracting men to me, for instance, even when there were spare seats in the train men would often choose to sit next to me. I now understood the sexual abuse I had carried in my spirit gave others the signal they could also abuse me.

A few days later, on Good Friday, the Holy Spirit opened my eyes anew to the real significance of the Cross. Jesus endured the pain and trauma, shame and rejection, darkness and death, so that I might cry out with Him, 'It is finished' (John 19:30). Jesus took the abuse for me. In my place He took death's burden and brought my abuse to an end on the Cross. He is truly my Saviour and Redeemer.

9 *Healing And Brokenness*

Over the next few months the Holy Spirit continued to work gently with me, bringing much cleansing. After the exposure and release of the rape a wide variety of issues relating to my self-image and my womanhood could be put in order by Him. I saw a picture of myself, exhausted from a long journey, standing at the door of the throne room of heaven, gazing into my Father's eyes, keen to run to Him. Many of my robes were still dirty, but this time I only needed to stand there whilst the angels at the door removed them.

In the rather daunting awareness that my journey was 'complete' I began my routine of inner healing once more. But this time the focus was not on the waves of memories and pain from the past. Instead I felt as if I was being equipped for the healthy living of my future. I began to learn how to read my feelings and co-operate with them on a daily basis. It meant listening to my spirit and to the Lord, rather than controlling my life with my mind. I deliberately practised treasuring my spiritual nature rather than squashing it under an assault of rationality.

A significant area of cleansing that the Lord brought to me during these months was in my attitude to life. I had lived for so many years in death that I had actually become quite comfortable in it. Sometimes I could feel the death in my body, especially my womb. At other times it was in my emotion, becoming despondent and listless. The Holy Spirit was persistent in seeking it out. Where the death rested, He could not reside. I chose to welcome life. Then some months later I chose to receive it more actively by deciding to take responsibility for living each day to the full. The concept of 'enjoying life' was a strange one and again needed a specific decision. Jesus not only wanted me to live, but wanted me to enjoy living.

My times of homework turned into spiritual health checks, which I promised the Lord I would undertake as often as necessary. Sometimes I would discover that I was really uptight and responding angrily, for no apparent reason. At other times I would be cooking supper, or sitting in the bath and suddenly start crying. I learnt to read these as clues, noting that it was time for another check-up. I would set aside time to sit before the Lord and ask the Holy Spirit to show me what was troubling me, so that I could give it to Him to cleanse. I had to practice, to learn how to hear the Holy Spirit and co-operate with the cleansing. Early on I had to give time several evenings a week to this process. As the months passed it settled down until eventually I could do it even in the midst of other activities. Some were related to situations of the day, people who had been the channel of attack, others to relationships I was finding difficult. Or perhaps the Holy Spirit was stirring a memory from my past, maybe healing a behaviour pattern. I was still very vulnerable, easily bruised by apparently routine events. My emotions became the true indicator of any damage which specifically needed to be brought to the Holy Spirit for His healing.

Walking With Christ

I learnt the importance of keeping a short account with God, not allowing sin or disorder to build up in my life. Having found a release from my past, day-to-day cleansing was necessary to walk freely with Christ and continue to hear

> *His voice clearly. Carrying yesterday's baggage makes us vulnerable to the Enemy. Although God has given us an eternal and indestructible spirit, our body is always vulnerable to attack. What God desires for all of us is that we let go of the sin and disorder of our pasts so that we are less exposed. We may not be able to stop Satan attacking us, but we are able to minimise the damage. Sin is spiritual disease and will make us sick and vulnerable, giving the Enemy authority to hurt us. The sooner we deal with it in humility, the better!*

The lies and purposes of the Enemy did not just disappear. At times I could still hear him beckoning me with his persuasive call. But these voices were now just whispering in my ear rather than reverberating in my head. So I learnt more and more to disentangle myself from them, as part of my on-going spiritual discipline.

Such personal check-ups have now become a way of life. It is the way the Holy Spirit helps me to keep myself spiritually and emotionally clean. During these audits He can talk to me about areas of my life He is displeased with, or where the Lord is not honoured in my attitudes or relationships. Without such times my sensitivity becomes dulled and my responses get confused, as they are influenced by outside issues. In my spirit I get out of tune with the Holy Spirit.

And so my journey became one of discovery – who was I after the baggage had gone? I asked myself what my potential really was, my place in the Body of Christ, the direction of my professional career – the questions seemed endless. I had by now grown accustomed to hearing from the Lord about myself, but discovered that He began talking to me about others and about the church. I found a reality in prayer that I had never imagined possible, as I was able to ask the Lord first what He wanted and then intercede in the understanding that His will would be done. For some months I had been helping to support others in need of similar ministry, and this now grew and grew. In worship, to my amazement, I discovered I could put my classical clarinet training to one side and play by ear. And I could worship freely in song too. This was a time of new beginnings.

I handed my four bedroomed house back to its owners – it had served me well for several years – and moved back to live with Mum. But this time the relationship was different. I was free from the female bloodline. Again the Lord began to focus on my womanhood. But here was a surprise. I had never enjoyed being a girl, preferring trousers and football. I assumed in my healing that would change – that my femininity would begin to grow. I would surely begin to enjoy babies, social relationships, make-up and clothes. But God had a deeper truth to reveal. I discovered a concept about manhood and womanhood that gave me permission not to try to meet the stereotype of sexuality that I had grown up with in the church, but just be myself.

The Gender Continuum

Peter introduced me to a simple but liberating concept. Imagine a straight line with male at the far left end and female at the right. In the middle is a line at right angles, representing the point where male ends and female begins. The far left is the macho Rambo-type male and the extreme right the very feminine woman. Just to the left of centre is the female-type man and just to the right the male-type woman, not in sexual orientation, but in gifting, skill and ability. Peter asked me where I was on this line. I thought for a time and began to realise I was on the extreme male end of female. I had a male type mind in a female body! This explained a lot, as I knew I could have been a good engineer, lawyer or accountant. Even neurobiology has now confirmed these strengths and weaknesses are mirrored in

> *the shape of our brain. I enjoyed knowing how machinery worked and was later very excited owning a classic Morris 1000 convertible. I began to see that God was not asking me to fit into a female mould, but just be myself. As we each become like Christ, we become more our unique selves.*

I understood for the first time in my life that I was not a people-oriented person. I did not find social contact stimulating, but draining. I enjoyed my own company. I was fascinated more by the heavy plant and logistics of road works than by beautiful views. This was not a perversion, not part of my baggage. It was simply who I was – I should not feel guilty! I still needed to learn to love people as Christ did, to give myself freely in relationship. But I did not need to pretend to be someone I wasn't. In allowing more of myself to be released I was free for the first time to choose to grow in what I liked and disliked. This was self-discovery.

Even at this stage in my healing, however, the Lord still had some surprises in store for me. I was most disappointed to discover that my humanity really began to show! Prior to my healing I had lived so intensely on huge amounts of adrenaline, that much of the time I was in a state of hyperstress. I had everything under tight control. Professionally and even in my former church, I had been able to do many things at once and do most of them exceptionally well. But the Lord had freed me from the driving forces of the baggage in my spirit. I had no idea of the 'energy' it had actually given me, until it had gone. In being introduced to myself I came down to earth with a thump! I made mistakes, got tired and was angry when I did not intend to be. I had assumed that the instability in my emotion would go away when I was healed, but instead I discovered that even healthy emotion can be unpredictable. That was quite a shock. It took me a while to realise that instead of becoming a super-saint after so much healing, I had been freed to be more human. I was becoming the person that the Lord had created me to be and only time and self-discipline would bring the maturing in my emotion and my spirit that I sought.

I began to take responsibility for who I was and who I wanted to be. It was a struggle, full of ups and downs. It took time. I had to 'own' myself, by accepting who I was, by receiving the Susan God had created me to be. The potential remained to move back into self-rejection. I found some aspects of me that I did not like, but were actually God-given. There was also some of me I did like that the Lord was taking away because He did not. With a shock I realised that the end result of healing is not that we become who we want to be. Rather we become who the Lord had always intended us to be. And there is a difference! I had never wanted the bundle of volatile healed emotion that God had given me. But I learnt that these feelings are one of the most reliable means He has of talking to me! I admired the intellectual ability I had, yet saw how often my mind got in God's way... The learning continued.

I did resent these ambushes from the Lord – it felt as if He was changing the ground rules. But I had come to the end of my journey of healing. I was free from my past. My 'problems' were no longer the focus of my life or my relationship with God. I could get on with living. And so I did. I even sat down and wrote the first draft of this manuscript – a testimony to the remarkable work of the Lord in my life.

But what comes after healing? I didn't know. The surgeon is never closer to the patient than when He is operating... did that mean I would not know the reality of the Lord's touch in the same way again? Would I become one of those Christians who had an encounter with Christ at one time in their life (albeit an encounter that lasted four years) and then spend the rest of their life testifying to it? These questions puzzled me in the following months. What next?

I began to drift in my relationship with God, to lack focus now that I had the healing I had sought. It took some time to admit that the healed woman that I was had no instinctive heart-felt desire to know God. Outwardly, the semblance of intimacy with Him was still there and I had a lot more understanding of His ways. On the whole I did not fall back into any of the deathly habits and life-styles I had so recently been freed from. But neither did I move forward into possessing and enjoying the fullness of my healing. The little I had of God was so much more than many around me and I was no longer in need. I was serving the Body of Christ, hearing from God clearly, but...

I was struggling with things that had never been a problem before I was healed. I was an angry person and now that I could feel what was in my spirit, my dislike of others, my impatience, my hard-heartedness were plain for all to see. Even to speak in a civil manner to my colleagues at work was often difficult. In the first ten years of my Christian life I spent all my time 'loving' and serving others. But with much of the baggage gone, I discovered I preferred to sit at my computer than help someone in need. I was not able to feed on the Word and receive life in my spirit. And whereas in my sickness I spent hours seeking God, I now found myself so angry with God that I did not want to spend time with Him. The anger was not evil, so where did it come from?

Things came to a head as I returned from a two-week summer 'holiday' as part of a mission team to Albania. I began to see that I had closed my mind and spirit to the Lord's truth. And in doing so I had allowed all kinds of lies and feelings to become a mass of anger and pain, most of which I directed at God. I actually believed God was dealing unjustly with some, if not all, of the situations I was facing. He was not treating me fairly. I had paid such a high price for my healing and He was not now doing His part. The more angry I became, the more I was convinced of the injustice of which I thought I was a victim. This continued for several months.

Over Christmas I began desperately pleading with God to meet with me. I could not continue in this way. Graciously the Lord began to show me the real problem. I was devastated to realise that in the first year of being able to enjoy my healing I had not pursued the Lord with all my heart. Much of my healing was still sitting on the shelf, untouched, unpossessed. For the next two weeks the Lord showed me many examples of areas of my life in which I was not living His way. I grew more depressed and more bewildered as I saw my fear and unwillingness to move in His ways. At the end of that two weeks, as I had begun to learn again to listen to Him and desire His ways more than my own, He brought the revelation of the real cause of the problem. I was angry that God was not giving me what I wanted. It was personal pride.

For the first couple of days I was stunned. Surely I had dealt with pride some time ago? But the Lord had decided in His wisdom that the beginning of this year and six years after my healing began, was the time when I should be introduced to the real me. He had brought radical healing in my life. He had intervened remarkably and rescued me from the purposes of Satan and the damage done by others. He had freed me to become the person He created me to be and had given me self-acceptance. But I had thought that person, the fruit of the Lord's work of healing would be beautiful. Instead, I was horrible! The whole drive of my healing had been to allow the Lord to release me to be 'me'. But I had totally ignored the fact that even the freed person the Lord created was contaminated and perverted by sin. After throwing out all the garbage I did not want, I was left with only myself – a self that stood opposed to God. With so much evil oppression I had not been free to see or be myself. But now I was meeting my true self – who I was without Jesus or the evil. I thought the person I was becoming free to be would be worth having. But I saw only an angry, self-centred, ugly and rebellious individual – my true state outside of Christ. The Lord was showing me that the person I really was, was diametrically opposed to the person I thought I had become.

Our False Selves

By the time we come to Christ, whatever our age, we will have inadvertently made extensive changes to God's blueprint of who He intended us to be. We will all have begun living for self, because living any other way makes us too vulnerable. Likewise our openness will have got us into too much trouble while our sensitivity will have been swamped by a brittle exterior. In all of this the person we have become, albeit false, is who we think we really are. We clothe that person with Christianity and church as we earnestly pursue our personal faith and growth.

What I had to learn was that if we let the Lord truly have His way, He will dismantle these false selves to expose our buried true self. But as we begin this journey, in time, we discover even our true self is a victim of the fall of man, defiled by its death and sinful decay. Only with the help of Christ can we call out our true self, allowing us to become who we were created to be. I began to see that we become like Christ as we become our true self in Christ.

As I recovered from the shock of discovering I had pride in my life, I was even more shocked to realise I was totally unwilling to give it up. My reaction was that I would rather turn around and walk away, abandon my future, my healing and my relationship with the Lord than give up my pride. It was very firmly established. I even felt I needed it, to bolster my ego and continue to believe in myself. It was self-congratulatory and I enjoyed the pat on the back it gave me. I did not feel sorry it was there, even though I knew that it had grieved my Lord and driven me away from Him. I was ashamed of my response, but it was an honest one. I preferred the pride. I preferred my self to the Lord.

Everything in me rebelled against letting go of my pride. The decision took several days to permeate into my spirit and several months to implement. Only slowly did I begin to desire the Lord I had chosen. I had to start by deliberately choosing to repent, even before I felt the sin of what I was doing. As I began repenting I realised pride had contaminated every area of my life. I began to battle with its lies, its uprightness, its mocking. Everywhere I looked I saw my pride staring back at me. At work I saw and began to hate my pride in my professional skills and in the successful business of which I was a part. Helping a friend with a prayer letter I suddenly despised the pride I felt when we did it well. My attitude to other women who had children or did not work was full of pride. And in my attitude to men I found a contempt which lied about the superiority of womanhood. The revelations of the areas of pride were incessant and overwhelming.

Part of the root of my pride was a bloodline inheritance. The righteous belief in self was firmly established in my family and was fed by a need to protect self from hurt imposed by others. It was a well-chosen defence mechanism that I had adopted as my own. Some parts of the pride were manipulative and controlling. Others were tenacious and stubborn.

I found the pride was intimately entangled with my relationship with God. I believed that if God had gone to so much effort to heal me I had to be someone special. I considered myself better than anyone else. And although I had been looking for love and a growing intimacy with the Lord even this stemmed from self-interest, fed by pride. The Lord knew that no intimacy with Him would be possible while my life was full of self. Love rooted in pride is not love for Him. It opposes and shuts out the Holy Spirit. Mercilessly it seemed, the Lord began to expose to me the motivation which undergirded my relationship with Him. It was something *I* did, *I* achieved, *I* worked at. I began to see that underneath all that work, if I stopped pursuing my relationship with God my way, I really didn't want one. If I couldn't do it the way I thought it should be done, I couldn't be bothered with God at all. With an intensely painful clarity I saw my arrogant rebellion against my Maker, my refusal to bow the knee before my Lord. How fickle to have pursued my healing, received so much from the Lord and then forget it all the instant self is about to be unseated.

I was puzzled to realise that the Lord had actually made use of my pride in the journey of healing. Having begun from a point of utter desperation, I had been too proud and selfish to give up the healing before I knew there was no more to receive. My tenacity in the pursuit of healing was rooted in a pride-full self-interest and self-survival. It is typical of the Lord to make use of all that stands against Him in His plans and purposes, before turning His holy light upon it to expose it.

The bombardment of self-discovery I was undergoing was leading me to plead before the Lord for His release of brokenness. The persistent cry of my heart was that there is no good thing in me. The passionate intensity of my depravity was overwhelming. I could not imagine how to live in brokenness – but I could not live any more the way I was. If I could not be broken, then I did not want to live, for any other way of life was becoming abhorrent to me.

Night after night I would return home from work to become engulfed in remorse, guilt and repentance, ashamed that I could still give self any place in my life.

But on the other hand, how could I live without the strength and protection self gave me? I wanted to provide for myself and have something to offer the Lord. Pride would not allow Him to provide for me, for I would need to relinquish self-control. My 'healthy self-image' was so interwoven with pride that I could not imagine feeling good about myself without it. My mind could not comprehend how to feel good about anything without being proud of it. I began to cry, pleading with God for the brokenness that only He could release. But instead of brokenness, I was becoming full of self-hate, with an arrogant refusal to talk to anyone or serve anyone because of the terrible person I really was. As I chose the Lord, I uncovered a holy fear of God, which propelled me away from His presence as I saw more of my own sin. Surely I could not come close to Him when I was this dirty? Fear meant I could not trust, and without trust in God how could I lay down pride?

What Is Brokenness?

I have often been asked this question and can only answer the way it was for me. Seeing my sin began a shift in my spirit toward a deeper allegiance to Christ. I saw I was not worthy of His life and love. This broke me. I felt so wretched – it brought me to an end of myself. I was in despair at my sin, unworthiness and yet His incessant love for me. In my complete vulnerability I found a new bonding of my spirit with His Holy Spirit. From that time I knew if I remained in this place of knowing personal unworthiness toward Him, His Spirit and mine together would cover my sinful fallen humanness and keep my arrogant prideful mind in place under it. For me it was the ascendancy of my spirit and His Spirit together taking their rightful place in my life, dislodging the arrogance of my mind and all its judgmental pride. Since that time I have had to live with the tension that on the one hand I am no more than 'a worm', while also being seated with Christ in eternal companionship with Him. This is the beginning of our real life in Christ, knowing meekness of spirit.

One measure of my opposition to any work of the Lord in my life regarding my pride was the deceit I would fall into when the Lord began to touch it. In the midst of the revelation about my self, I found pride up to even more tricks. I was becoming proud of how terrible I was! I was about to be proud of my brokenness. And even when I spotted this and repented, I became absorbed in death and repentance, totally losing sight of the fact that brokenness would lead me into His life. I preferred wallowing in the death of pride to the opening of my spirit to Christ and choosing life. In the deceit of pride I decided that I had no relationship with God and I began to give my time to grieving for its absence. But even this was a lie, luring me into a self-pitying introversion which was self-deception.

The Lord invited me to begin pondering who I was in His eyes as I knelt at the foot of the Cross, clothed in His righteousness. Several times He introduced me to this truth. To begin with it was unbearable. The sin I had so recently learnt to abhor became even worse when held up against His light. When I realised it was someone the Lord had created but whom I had so corrupted, the repentance I felt seemed very shallow. I wondered if I was becoming a Christian for the first time as I stood amazed at His love for someone such as me? It was easier for me to wallow in the mud of my old self, than to allow Him to clothe me in white. How could the Lord look upon me?

But the clarity of the truth was lost as I became consumed again in my own unworthiness, losing sight of Him who had brought me to this place. I was horrified at the persistent refusal of self to bow the knee, even after many decisions to choose brokenness. But unlike the power of evil, self never leaves. Its authority and influence is never finally broken in this life. Only slowly and very reluctantly did I begin to see that this battle with self trying to raise itself up is in fact never over. It was no good for me to keep fighting with pride, trying to put it down – that only gave self more of the attention it demanded. I had to stop waiting for the battle to end. I had to simply make a choice which I would be prepared to remake every day of my life, by God's grace. My choice is Christ and Him only.

The Lord was bringing me to an end of my self. For the first time in my life I knew I had nothing to offer Him and deserved nothing from Him save His eternal wrath. Nothing in myself that is good comes from me – what audacity even to think it. The beauty of the pot is given it by the potter and any usefulness it may have is likewise endowed. How could the creature rise up against the Creator in such rebellion?

The Journey Into Maturity

Over the years patterns have emerged of various stages of this road to wholeness. All of us begin with a selfish self-interest and motivation to sort ourselves out. We are all driven by our need. This first stage is for ourselves, a journey of healing of self, just as Christ did for all the pagan people that came to Him.

But the beginning of the second stage is when we have let go of the excess of our baggage and are becoming free to make a decision for Christ. His response to our willingness is to show us our sin, which will lead to brokenness if we let it. Many of us fight it. But this is where I have reached in the book. This second stage is for the

Lord, and will reveal to us who we really are and who He created us to be. This is the beginning of maturity.

This in turn leads to the final stage, for the Church, when we move into consistent spiritual gifting, able to discern good from evil (Hebrews 5:14), and carry the anointing of this knowledge. This is maturity in Christ.

The final step of the Lord dealing with my pride was a battle of surrender. I found I was unwilling to give myself to the Lord. I did not trust what He would do with me if I gave myself totally to Him. Graciously the Lord reminded me that all He wanted to do was clothe me in His white robes. But all the while I hold on in pride, He cannot give me these robes. He invited me to abandon myself to Him – my hopes and fears, my dreams and desires. He was not looking for a partnership – He wanted a takeover. I must lay all at His feet and in trust receive whatever He gives. Hopeless resignation is not honouring to Him. Only childlike trust gives Him His rightful place. For much of our lives we fight for some little piece of independence, some opportunity to make our mark in the world, some cause to stand for, or to rebel against. But my mark is not worth making and I give my independence up. I only want to have some small part in making the mark of the Lord and even that, only for Him.

The intensity of this final work of the Lord was astounding to me. I can think of no other issue that became so all-consuming as the Lord revealed self to me. For three months everywhere I looked I saw more of my pride and my utter inability to deal with it or live without it. There was no escape from it. And as the Lord began revealing Himself and His mercy, it felt too quick. I was frightened I had not learnt the lesson well enough and would return to my pride-full ways. But it is a daily decision to dethrone self and choose Christ. Without it we are lost.

Life And Death

Enjoying life means being aware of the amount of death around us. For growth and further life is only released in pain, tears and death. I began to see a little of this profound spiritual paradox. Where there is death, there is potential of new life. Life and death, death and life. They must both walk the road together. But the death of self I must carry in secret so that I can be the channel of Christ's life to others.

In Satan's kingdom there is plenty of death, but no life. Satan cannot create life, he seeks only the destruction of it. But in the Kingdom of God, there is never life without a prior death. The journey that the Lord had taken me through for the previous five years had first required my death, in order that I could receive His life. And it was Jesus' death that had won me life. Life and death – death is where true life is birthed. The Bible makes it very clear that it is what we lay down and allow to die that God can breathe life into. That which we cling on to possessively for ourselves is what will bring us death or loss. Enjoyment of life requires we also taste and feel death.

So what is God's way? – that like a little child I open my heart and my hands and receive from Him gratefully and thankfully. I choose to receive whatever He chooses to give – be it blessing from His abundance or barrenness for my refining. Likewise I must choose to give life to others. I have nothing to give save what He gives me. But giving to others does not mean acquiescing to them in slavery – giving means giving the person that my Lord has given me to be. Giving to others can only begin after we have given ourselves to Christ. Satan whispers that when we lose our independence, we lose ourselves. The Holy Spirit responds that when we completely surrender, only then can we find our true place in Christ. In Christ and in surrender my will becomes free for the first time, and whilst I lay aside pride and self I become free to choose righteously for Christ. It is the only place where my will can be in harmony with my Lord's.

There is now a daily battle for my heart to stay soft. Some days it is more intense than others, but every day there is a choice – will I give ground to self, or will I choose only Christ? The pride and rebellion of self will not die, but will raise its head in many and varied ways. But every time it is exposed it must be dragged kicking and screaming to a place of submission under the blood of Christ. Brokenness is only released by daily decisions to give myself completely to my Lord. Dealing with pride never feels good. Self will never go willingly to its place of submission, and my feelings are forever too closely attached to that prideful self. So, unlike dealing with the demonic, there is no 'breath of fresh air' when my self is crucified and Christ is allowed to reign. It is a decision of faith.

This barren place is the beginning of my rest in Christ, knowing that I have no strength and no ability even to be obedient by my own strength. I have nothing to give save a tired, damaged, refusing-to-be-broken shadow of who I was created to be. I give up the fight. I lay down my self with its incestuous idolatry, kneeling before His Lordship. Only by You Lord is self dethroned, for You to be given Your rightful place. Be it barrenness or bounty I *will* love you. I welcome Your take-over of my life. I have nothing to offer. Let me be content Lord, to be only, ever Yours.

Having now ventured with the Lord into many of the rooms of my spiritual house I began to see some were now the way He intended them to be. He had closed the windows so the Enemy could not trespass any longer. He had begun filling my house with His radiant presence and I am beginning to make it my home. But then He pauses. The Lord has given me what He promised, to take my past so I can possess a future. But He now asks the question, do I want it to be my house or His? If I want to give my house over to him, then a whole new journey must begin, a journey exploring in wholeness the person He created me to be. This next stage of my journey begins by my giving Him back what He has already given to me. This I have chosen to do, Lord God.

10 *The Purpose Of Healing*

'Rise up, my princess,' I heard Him say. Surely this could not be the Lord. Never before had I heard someone speak such a tender invitation. Must be my imagination. But I carried on 'imagining'. I had been quite agitated and grieved over a new layer of my own sin and the pain it caused those I loved. I felt as if He spoke to four men, with compassion in His eyes; 'She is too weak to move. Carry her to the bed.' The angels lifted me to a place of safety and began gently removing the festering coverings, to expose my wounds. For the first time ever, I felt no fear at the approach of His love. I could rest. I knew that next time He approached, I would not need to bow at His feet, but was at last ready to welcome His embrace.

Gradually it dawned on me that this was not an event that was happening to me. Rather the Lord was painting a cameo of the journey He had taken me through in the previous years of healing. It was a journey of pain, of truth and of intimacy with the Lord, all simultaneously.

What is God's ultimate goal in fighting for our healing and wholeness? I had always known that the Lord wanted to free me to be the person He had created. This, I assumed, was because of His love for me that I might glorify Christ. But I have come to see a deeper, fuller purpose in my healing. It has nothing to do with service or gifting or calling and everything to do with the Father's love for the Son. Only when free from the baggage which was weighing me down could I become free to love and exalt the Son, giving

Him His rightful place. Only in my freedom from the power of death can I know the victory won by the Lord Jesus on the Cross. Only in tasting life can I appreciate the sacrifice of the King of life who tasted death so that I could live.

In being healed I am then equipped to love the Son. In being healed the Father can then begin to share with me the intimate passion He has for His Son. The Father does not only want me to become like His Son. He wants me to be absorbed in anointed zeal for His Son, which lifts the Son ever higher. As I grow in love for Jesus I myself am made ready, as part of the Church, to be the Bride which the Father is preparing to give to His Son. That has been the true purpose of my healing and the reason God has given so much time and energy to it. It is what He desires for all His children, that without distraction, in adoration, we might *freely* worship and exalt the Lord Jesus Christ.

And in discovering how the Lord wanted to heal me and set me free, I have had an equipping to stand with others which is immeasurable. Not only can I speak from a wealth of experience with those who have areas of damage from which they want to be free, but I can now hear the Lord with a clarity and precision for them which I had never imagined possible. In the wave of international evangelism which must characterise this first decade of the new millennium, we must offer young Christians the means to be free from years of abuse, betrayal, fear, guilt, hate, revenge, shame – free to become who they were created to be.

Our Stolen Spiritual Potential

One of the interesting ideas that I began to see worked out in my life was the concept that we carry in our spirit, from our earliest days, the potential we could realise in the Holy Spirit. The person we can become in Christ is already a potential reality. But it seems Satan is also somehow aware of this future. His destructive intent is to steal that potential, ensuring it is never realised. He will attempt to prevent us from ever inviting Christ into our lives. And his damage will target areas of our gifting and potential anointing, so that even if we become the Lord's, our real capacity to harm him and be effective in Christ is never achieved.

As we prepare for the battles of the Last Days, we must allow our Lord to prepare for Himself an army able to stand. I believe we can each reach a place in Christ now where although we cannot stop the attack, we can prevent the damage. We must be able to withstand in Christ the attacks of Satan, in purity and humility. We must allow God to cleanse and redeem, to mingle His Holy Spirit freely with our spirits, untying those knots that make us casualties even before the real warfare begins. May we learn from Him how to make ourselves and each other free and ready for the spiritual battles. Father God, let the Bride be readied for the Bridegroom.

> 'Worthy is the Lamb, who was slain,
> to receive power and wealth and wisdom and strength
> and honour and glory and praise!'
> (Revelation 5:12)

THANKS BE TO GOD.

THE NEXT STEP ...

Perhaps by reading this book issues have been stirred up for you but you do not know what to do next. Or maybe you can relate in some way to Susan's own experiences and are needing help. Or you could be one of those to whom the Lord has been speaking but you do not know what to do with the knowledge.

If so, we would like to suggest one or more of the following:

BEGIN DOING "HOMEWORK": We encourage folk to spend an hour a day just waiting on the Lord and allowing Him to talk to them. As He does you will need to then apply what He says to your own life. To help you with this 'hands on approach' we hold regular workshops.

JEHOVAH RAPHA WORKSHOPS: These are held both here in the UK and abroad so please write to us, as we will be pleased to give you details should you wish to attend one of them. They are inexpensive, practical and have proven very effective with hundreds of folk in the past. Don't be fearful, give us a call.

WOULD YOU LIKE A WORKSHOP IN YOUR AREA OR CHURCH? If you would like to explore this possibility then please give us a call or drop us a line with what you have in mind.

THE BOOK *Passion for Purity* is available for sale if you would like to make a gift of it to a friend who you believe could be helped by it. Contact us at the address below.

"COFFEE MEETINGS": We could hold a coffee morning or evening in your area to introduce our ministry to your friends. If you can get twenty to thirty of your friends together and are interested in exploring this idea, please give us a call. Otherwise we would be pleased to send you a free tape of such a meeting.

BE PUT ON OUR MAILING LIST: We have an international mailing list that will keep you up-to-date with events in our ministry. If you would like to be kept informed please give us a call or drop us a line.

VISIT CHRIST CHURCH DEAL: If you live close enough to join us for church then feel free to visit our fellowship on a Sunday morning. Ring the telephone number below for details.

ARE YOU ONE OF THE LONG-TERM MENTALLY ILL, LIKE SUSAN WAS?: We run a specialist programme for selected clients to help them break the habit of prescribed drugs. Or you may have reached a place of despair either in your local church or personal life. Alternatively, you may be in long-term care but feel you still have not fully explored the reasons why you are ill. Please note you do not have to be a committed Christian to either talk to us or be helped by us. But if you feel we can be of help to you, we would be pleased to talk through your situation and see what can be done. In the first instance please write to us with some of your background, or call the office during office hours. All contacts will be treated in strict confidence.

DISCIPLESHIP LTD
Waterfront
Kingsdown Road
Walmer
Kent, CT14 7LL
England

Tel/fax : 01304 239621
EMail : waterfront@btinternet.com